Better Spanish

Better Spanish

Achieving Fluency
through everyday speech

Carole Shepherd

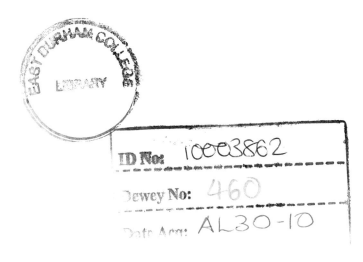
© 2008 by Carole Shepherd
additional material © 2007 Studymates Limited.

ISBN: 978-1-84285-089-3

First published in 2008 by Studymates Limited.
PO Box 225, Abergele, LL18 9AY, United Kingdom.

Website: http://www.studymates.co.uk

Typeset by Vikatan Publishing Solutions, Chennai, India
Printed and bound in Europe

Contents

Preface | xi

1 Choosing the correct verb | **1**
One-minute overview | 1
Cocinar, cocer, guisar – *to cook* | 2
Coger, tomar, pillar – *to catch* | 3
Comenzar, empezar, principiar – *to begin* | 4
Decir, contar – *to say* | 5
Dejar, salir, abandonar, quedar – *to leave* | 6
Echar, lanzar, tirar, arrojar – *to throw* | 7
Echar de menos/extrañar, perder(se),
     fallar – *to miss* | 10
Gastar, pasar – *to spend* | 12
Gustar, querer, tener cariño, encantar,
     interesar, parecer – *to (be) like* | 12
Ir, salir, funcionar, marchar – *to go* | 14
Jugar, tocar, actuar – *to play* | 15
Luchar, combatir, pelear, pugnar – *to fight* | 16
Morir, fallecer, fenecer – *to die* | 18
Necesitar, hacer falta,
     requerir – *to need, require* | 19
Poner, colocar, meter – *to put* | 20
Probar, intentar, tratar de, ensayar,
     cansar – *to try* | 21
Querer, necesitar, desear, esperar, – *to want* | 23
Saber, conocer, reconocer, informarse,
     enterarse – *to know* | 23
Ser, estar, haber – *to be* | 25
Tener – *to have* | 26
Tomar, coger, llevar, sacar, cobrar – *to take* | 27
Usar, emplear, utilizar, servirse de,
     aprovechar, agotar – *to use* | 29
Helping you learn | 31

2 Choosing the right word - 1 | **33**
One-minute overview | 33
Adjectives: the right word for *brown*, | 33
     free | 34
     old | 35

slim   37

wrong   38

Nouns: the right word for *country*   40

face   41

half   42

help   43

speed   44

time   45

work   46

Connectors: the right word for *and,*   48

but,   48

for,   49

or   51

so   51

Helping you learn   54

3 Choosing the right word - 2   **55**

One-minute overview   55

Everyday false friends *(falsos amigos)*   55

Less common false friends   63

Helping you learn   70

4 Practising awkward words and phrases - 1   **71**

One-minute overview   71

Tag questions   71

Repetition   72

Exclamations   73

Common useful phrases   76

Helping you learn   78

5 Practising awkward words and phrases - 2   **79**

One-minute overview   79

Some awkward words and their translations   79

Awkward words with a cultural explanation   80

Common idioms   87

Helping you learn   96

6 The force of "four-letter" words   **97**

One-minute overview   97

Difference of meaning – and ferocity! – of
these words in the Spanish-speaking world 97
Helping you learn 102

**7 Using Spanish correctly
and with fluency   103**
One-minute overview 103
Pronunciation in general 103
The purity of vowels 104
The pronunciation of certain consonants 104
The use of the written accent 107
Use of the diminutive 109
Double and final consonants 109
Intonation 109
Latin American usage 110
Unspoken fluency 111
Helping you learn 113

8 Mastering difficult structures   115
One-minute overview 115
The use of personal *a* 115
The use of *ahora bien* 116
The use of the articles 116
The use of adjectives 123
The use of collective nouns 126
The use of impersonal verbs 127
The importance of sentence structure 128
The use of the subjunctive mood 130
The use of prepositions and their
associated verbs 134
Specific translation pitfalls 140
Helping you learn 143

Websites for students of Spanish 145

Appendix: A brief linguistic history
of a beautiful language 151

Index of English words 155

Index of Spanish words 156

About the Author 158

Foreword

The student of any foreign language is confronted by a near impossible task: to telescope into a few years, at most, a process which takes the native speaker a whole lifetime of constant bombardment with language, years and years of immersion in their country and its language and culture. Learning a foreign language at school or as an adult means having to take shortcuts, and to rely on the key elements of language—grammar, vocabulary and usage—being fed to you in large bite-size chunks, rather than being drip-fed over a lifetime as a native-speaker. Most students rely on good textbooks, grammars, vocabulary books and dictionaries; the student of Spanish is fortunate in having a wide range of such books from which to choose. However, one important area for which little material exists is that of usage: whilst a good dictionary will provide the necessary 'feel' for discreet words and phrases, and appropriate examples of usage, little material exists which is capable of imparting a broader feel for this most important element of a language. This new Studymates Guide distils this feel into one well-structured and information-packed volume. It provides the student of Spanish with a vital insight into the subtleties and richness of spoken Spanish: as such it is an extremely valuable aid to the student who aspires to fluency.

In my experience, the best language teachers are those whose infectious enthusiasm and interest for their subject leads them to develop a *persona* which owes more to the language and culture they teach than to their own origins. The best language books are those written by such teachers, whose years of experience have shown them what works best with their students. In this book Carole Shepherd reveals her great enthusiasm for Spanish, and offers the student the benefit of her many years of ongoing study of the Spanish language in all its glory, and of her years of successful teaching.

This volume will be an enormous asset to the student who wishes to acquire fluency through an awareness of authentic usage. Its contribution is all the more valuable in the case of a vibrant language like Spanish, a true world language with a terrific richness and variety of vocabulary and idiom, in which one simple word or expression has a wide range of nuances depending on which part of the Hispanic world you happen to be in!

Mike Zollo
– TUTOR, Nelson Thornes Distance Learning;
Chief examiner AQA AS/A2 Spanish;
formally Head of Modern Languages,
Britannia Royal Naval College,
Dartmouth,
Devon

Preface

This new Studymate is aimed at higher-level students of Spanish from GCSE onwards and anyone with an interest in speaking the language to a reasonable level of fluency.

Spanish is a beautiful language which is rich in vocabulary and as expressive as the people who speak it. For the non-native speaker, the potential pitfalls of speaking Spanish fluently are often found not in a lack of vocabulary per se but rather in the choice of words made because some undergo a subtle change of meaning in different contexts.

It is an understanding of these possible changes of meaning, not to mention any invaluable help and explanations from Spanish-speaking friends which can be gleaned along the way, which ultimately puts a non-native speaker on the road to successful fluency.

It should also be borne in mind that some words and expressions, particularly in spoken language, can be somewhat 'here today and gone tomorrow'. So another potential stumbling block when trying to gain fluency in any language is to be aware that words which are 'hip' today are 'cool' the next and 'mega' the day after! Try not to see this as preventing you from unlocking the door to fluency, but rather as an enrichment of a language as it is really spoken.

This guide, therefore, aims to provide an insight into the subtleties and richness of spoken Spanish, not a watertight answer to all problems! Treat it as a complement to your dictionary and grammar books and don't be afraid to experiment. A spoken language is a living thing and Spanish is one of the most vibrant of all. Keep it alive, enjoy it and remember: fluency is for the taking!

Acknowledgements: to all friends and family who have endured my tenser moments!; to the staff of Virgo Fidelis Convent Senior School in Croydon for their technical support and input; to the pupils of the same for their endurance, their willingness to be a part of experimental testing of theories, their constantly positive approach towards my goal, and their co-operation in helping me to achieve it; to Leo Hickey, University of Salford, for invaluable teaching in the early stages of my career and for support to date; and to Mike Zollo and Phil Turk for their grammatical influence.

Carole Shepherd

1 Choosing the correct verb

One-minute overview

Choosing the correct verb is a big step on the fluency ladder and, as with most aspects of language learning, getting the *meaning* right is a major part of the learning curve. For example, 'to play' is *jugar* when translated in a general sense of playing with something or at a sport or game. However, when musical instruments are being played we need the verb *tocar*. A common error for many non-native speakers of Spanish occurs when using the verb 'to be', which can be translated by *ser*, *estar* or *haber*. Each one has its own subtle meanings and in some cases can be switched with one of the others in order to purposefully change that meaning!

This chapter will endeavour to explain some of these subtleties and clarify a few of the meanings of the following verbs:

- the correct verb for *to cook*
- the correct verb for *to catch*
- the correct verb for *to begin*
- the correct verb for *to say*
- the correct verb for *to leave*
- the correct verb for *to throw*
- the correct verb for *to miss*
- the correct verb for *to spend*
- the correct verb for *to like*
- the correct verb for *to go*
- the correct verb for *to play*
- the correct verb for *to fight*
- the correct verb for *to die*
- the correct verb for *to need*

- the correct verb for *to put*
- the correct verb for *to try*
- the correct verb for *to want*
- the correct verb for *to know*
- the correct verb for *to be*
- the correct verb for *to have*
- the correct verb for *to take*
- the correct verb for *to use*

Cocinar, cocer, guisar – *to cook*

Cocinar is the most *common* verb used for the English equivalent *to cook/to do the cooking.*

¿Sabes *cocinar*?   Do you know how to/can you *cook*?

Linked words are therefore:

La cocina (kitchen, or stove/cooker) and it can also refer to 'cuisine': *la cocina catalana* (Catalan cuisine); *la cocina casera* (plain/home cooking). Note also *un libro de cocina* (a cookery book).

Una cocinilla, a 'kitchenette/small kitchen' or, equally, a 'small stove/cooker'.

El/la cocinero/a is the person who does the cooking, the cook.

Cocer also means *to cook* but has the added meanings of *to boil* or *to steam cook, to fire* (in a kiln) or *to ferment* (of wine).

Linked words are:

La cocción (cooking/boiling). Note *el agua de cocción* (boiling water), which food can then be cooked in.

El cocido (a type of stew).

Guisar also means *to cook* but is equally used for *to stew*

Linked words are:

Un guisado.   A stew.

Un guiso.   A cooked dish/stew.

Un guisote is a pejorative usage. meaning 'hash/poor-quality stew' and can be compared to English words such as 'concoction/grub' but, again, with overtones of not being particularly palatable!

Also useful to know

1 **Preparar** can be used, in the context of food, to refer to the process of cooking something.

2 **Cocinar** can be used figuratively to mean 'to meddle':
Siempre estás *cocinando* algo.   You're so *nosey*!/You're always *looking for gossip*!/You're always *cooking up something*!

3 When used in the reflexive form, **cocerse** and **guisarse** mean 'to be brewing':
A ver, ¡que algo *se cuece*!   Watch out, something's *cooking* (there is a problem *brewing*).

4 The word **cocido** within other contexts can have its own meanings:
Estar cocido is 'to be hacked off/fed up about something' or, a bit more literally, 'to be roasting (hot)'
Ganarse el cocido is 'to earn one's living' (the idea being in order to eat).

5 Note that **guisante** (pea), although edible, has nothing to do with the way it is cooked.

6 **A guisa de/de tal guisa que** has nothing at all to do with cooking but rather they are prepositional phrases meaning 'as/like/in such a way that'.

Coger, tomar, pillar – *to catch*

Coger is usually used for *catching/taking/going by* some means of transport.

Vamos a *coger* el tren.   Let's *go by/catch* the train.
¿Cómo vas al trabajo? *Cojo* el metro.   How do you get to work? I *go by/catch* the tube.

Tomar has a variety of meanings but is mostly used to mean *to take/catch*.
Tomó bien la noticia.   He *took* the news well.
El susto *me tomó* el aliento.   The fright *made me catch* my breath.

No te puedo *toma*r en serio.   I can't *take* you seriously.
Tomo el autobús para ir al centro.   *I take/catch* the bus to
get to the town centre.

Pillar is slightly more colloquial than the previous two verbs
and means *to catch unawares*.
Le *pillé* al niño comiendo helado.   *I caught* the little boy
eating ice cream.
Se *pilló* los dedos en la puerta del coche.   *She caught* her
fingers in the car door.

Also useful to know

1   **Coger** can also be used for catching an illness or a prisoner,
    acquiring tickets or a job, or for being caught out.

2   **Tomar** generally means 'to take' but can also be used for
    eating and/or drinking (to substitute *comer/beber* or both).

3   **Pillar** can also mean 'to grasp/seize' and 'to knock down/
    run over'.
    Note that all three of these verbs can be used with a sexual
    connotation (see reference to *coger* on page 100).

Comenzar, empezar, principiar – *to begin*

Comenzar is used to mean *to begin/to start/to commence* and
is very often followed by a preposition or gerund:
Siempre comienzas discutiendo.   You always begin with
an argument.
¡Comienza a hacer el pingüino nada más entrar en casa!
He starts to act the fool as soon as he gets home!
Comenzar con/por.   To begin with/by.
Linked word:
El comienzo.   The start/beginning/onset.

Empezar is almost synonymous with *comenzar* and similarly
is often followed by a preposition or gerund:
Empezó a llover a cántaros.   *It began* pouring down/
raining cats and dogs.
El Presidente *empezó diciendo* que . . .   The President
began by saying . . .

Linked words:

El empiece.   The start/beginning.

El empiezo.   The Latin American equivalent of *comienzo*.

Principiar is less commonly used in its verb form but, when it is, it is used with the prepositions *a* and *con* and works in the same way as *comenzar* and *empezar*. More commonly it is the linked words from this verb with which we are generally more familiar:

Principal.   Principal, main, foremost, first.

El principio.   The beginning, origin, early stage.

El/la principiante/a.   Beginner, novice.

Also useful to know

1 **Comienzo** and **principio** in the plural are commonly used to mean 'at the beginning of a period of time':
   En los comienzos/a principios de este siglo.   At *the turn/beginning* of the century.

2 **Empezar** is the one of the three most commonly used in the following situation:
   ¡No empieces!   Don't start (when said to a pre-tantrum child!) or Don't start again (when the person in question will not let a subject drop).

3 The word **principiante** can also have less favourable connotations of someone who is very naïve or 'wet behind the ears'/green or inexperienced.

4 The word **principio** also has other meanings, namely those of *moral principle* or *chemical element*:
   Es hombre de principios.   He is a man of *principle*.

Decir, contar – *to say*

Decir *commonly means to say/mean.*

Lo que he dicho.   I stand by what *I said*.

¡No me digas!   You don't say!/Really?/Get away!

¿Qué dices?   Whatever *do you mean*?/Whatever *are you saying*?

Se dice.   It is said/people say.

Contar means *to say* but very often gives the impression of doing so at unnecessary length; it also means *to tell/ recount.*

¿Qué me *cuentas?*   Whatever are *you saying* to me?

Cuéntame un cuento de hadas.   *Tell me* a fairy story.

No creo en todo lo que me *has contado.*   I don't believe all that *you've told/said* to me.

Also useful to know

1 **Digo**, the first person of **decir**, is used when you wish to correct something you have said ('I mean').

2 **Digo yo** is used for emphasis: ('**I** think'/'in **my** opinion').

3 **Díga(me)** is the conventional way of answering the telephone ('Hello?').

4 **Que digamos** can be used almost sarcastically to negate a comment:
No hace calor *que digamos* means exactly the opposite.

5 **Contar** can also mean 'to count'.

Dejar, salir, abandonar, quedar – *to leave*

Dejar is used for all general meanings of *to leave*, but also *to leave alone, to leave behind, to allow* and *to stop.*

¡*Déja*me en paz!   *Leave* me alone!

Dejar algo para mañana.   *To leave* something until tomorrow.

Deja mucho que desear.   *It leaves* a lot to be desired.

No me *dejan* hacerlo.   *They won't let* me do it.

Dejó de fumar hace ya un año.   *She stopped* smoking a year ago now.

He *dejado* mi lista de compras en casa.   *I've left* my shopping list at home.

Salir is used to mean *to leave* or *to go out.*

El tren con destino a Zamora *sale* a las ocho.   The Zamora train *leaves* at eight.

Salió de la casa a mediodía.   *He left* the house at midday.

Abandonar is used when the idea to be conveyed is *to leave out/leave behind* intentionally. It is much stronger than *dejar*.
Abandonaron a sus hijos en casa.   *They left* their children at home (implication is that it was done on purpose).
Cariño, me tienes *abandonada*.   Darling, you're *leaving me out/ignoring me*.

Quedar is used when the idea is of *being left over/ remaining*.
Después de las vacaciones me *queda* poco dinero.   I have little money *left* (over) after the holidays.
No me queda más remedio.   *I have no* alternative (left).
Prefiero *quedarme* en casa.   I prefer *to stay/be left* at home.

Also useful to know

1 **Dejar** can also be used in several self-contained phrases:
   Dejar caer.   To drop (to let fall).
   Dejar de + infinitive.   To stop (doing something).
   Dejar plantado.   To stand (someone) up.
   No *dejar* piedra por/sin mover.   To leave no stone unturned.

2 **Quedar** can also mean 'to fit/suit' (of clothes); 'to appear' (of people); and 'to indicate distance or position' (of a place).

3 **Quedar** also means 'to remain' or 'to be in a certain emotional or physical state' when referring to people.

4 **Quedar** also comes with set phrases:
   ¿En qué *quedamos*?   So what *are we doing*?
   Se quedó en nada.   *It came* to nothing.

Echar, lanzar, tirar, arrojar – *to throw*

Echar has many meanings along the lines of *to throw*: *to fling, to cast, to shower, to eject, to throw out* but also many other meanings which can be colloquial, idiomatic or simply just very different from the primary translation given in any one dictionary (see page 90).

Echar algo a un lado.   *To throw* something to one side (literally and figuratively).

Echar algo a cara o cruz.   To *toss up* for something.

Echar algo a suertes.   To *draw lots* for something.

Si protesta, ¡que le *echen* fuera!   If he makes a fuss, *chuck him out!*

Echar maldiciones.   To *shower* with curses.

Echa bien el cerrojo esta noche.   Make sure you *bolt* the door well tonight.

Echar la cabeza a un lado.   *To cock/tilt* one's head to one side.

Echar el muerto/la culpa a alguien.   To *lay the blame* on someone.

Echar a reír/correr.   To *burst out* laughing/to *break into* a run.

Lanzar, again, has several meanings but they are more closely connected with the verb *to throw*:

Lanzar un grito.   *To utter* a cry.

Lanzar un balón.   *To hurl* a ball.

Lanzar un desafío.   *To throw out/down* a challenge.

Also the commonest linked words give the idea of something in some way being *thrown* or even *launched*:

Una lanza.   Lance/spear.

Una lanzabombas.   Mortar.

Un lanzacohetes.   Rocket launcher.

Un lanzador.   Thrower/bowler/pitcher.

Un lanzallamas.   Flamethrower.

Lanzado/a.   Forward/brazen or determined/single-minded.

Tirar does, unfortunately, have other connotations (see page 103) but also means *to throw, to hurl, to knock over, to shoot, to launch, to take(photo), to throw away*:

Tirar la basura.   *To throw out* the rubbish.

Tiró un beso a su novia.   *He blew* his girlfriend a kiss.

Tirar a matar.   *To shoot* to kill.

Linked words:

Un/a tirador/a.   Marksman/shooter.

Arrojar, again, has the meanings *to throw, to hurl, to fling* and also *to throw out, to emit, to give out, to produce, to yield*:

A ver si tus ideas *arrojan* alguna luz sobre el tema.   Let's see if your ideas *throw/shed/cast* any light on the subject.
Arrojar algo de sí.   *To fling* something aside.
Linked words:
Arrojadizo/a.   (Of a weapon) used by being thrown.
Arrojado/a.   Daring, dashing, reckless (i.e. ready to throw yourself into something).
El arrojo.   Daring, fearlessness.
Con arrojo.   Boldly.

Also useful to know

1   All these verbs can be used reflexively, which inevitably gives them a different slant on their original meanings.

Echarse – 'to have/get', 'to fling/throw oneself' or 'to lie down/stretch out':
Me voy a echar un pitillo.   *I'm going for* a fag/*to have* a smoke.
Llegó el novio y la novia *se echó* en sus brazos.   When the boy arrived, his girlfriend *threw herself/fell into* his arms.
El gato *se echó* al sol.   The cat *lay down/stretched out* in the sun.

Lanzarse – 'to throw/fling/hurl oneself into/on', 'to rush/fly at' or 'to embark upon':
El león *se lanzó* a su víctima.   The lion *pounced* upon its prey.
El campeón *se lanzó* al agua.   The champion *dived* into the water.

Tirarse – 'to throw oneself', 'to dive/plunge', 'to lie down' or 'to spend (time) doing':
Se tiró tres horas con sus deberes de química.   *She spent* three hours on her chemistry homework.

Arrojarse – 'to throw/hurl oneself into/on/through' or 'to rush/fling oneself into':
Se arrojó en sus brazos y se echo a llorar.   *She threw herself* into his arms and began to cry.

2   **Echar** also has some more familiar meanings, which are mainly spoken:

¿Cuántos años le *echas*?   How old *do you reckon* he is?

¿Qué *echan* esta noche en la tele?   *What's on* TV tonight?

¿*Echamos* un cafetito?   *Fancy* a coffee?

¿Por qué no *echamos* por esta calle?   Why don't *we go* this way?

3 **Tirar** also can be used to mean almost the opposite of throwing when used to mean 'to pull/tug', 'to attract/draw', 'to get along/manage', 'to last' or 'to tend to/towards':

¡No me *tires* de la manga!   Don't *pull on* my sleeve!

No me tiran mucho las ciencias.   Science *doesn't do* much for me/I'm *not drawn* to Science.

¿Qué tal te va? *Tirando.*   How are you? *Getting by.*

Este abrigo de colegio *le tiene que tirar* otro invierno. That school coat *has to last her* another winter.

Mi madre *tira a* vieja.   My mother *is getting* old.

4 Also **tirar** can be used in the phrase **a toda tira** to mean 'at most/at the latest':

Llegará a las tres *a toda tira.*   He'll be here by three *at the latest.*

5 *Tirantes* is a linked word to these latter meanings of **tirar** as it means 'braces' *or* 'suspenders'. (idea of holding/pulling up)

Echar de menos/extrañar, perder(se), fallar – *to miss*

Echar de menos/extrañar - these two verbs are used when 'to miss' means 'to long for a person or a thing'

Cuando estoy viajando, *echo de menos* a mi gato.   When I am travelling *I miss* my cat.

Yo *extraño* mucho a mis animales domésticos también.   *I* also *miss* my pets . (This is more L. Am. usage.)

Perder(se) is used for *missing/being too late for* a form of transport. Also it can be used for *to lose*:

He perdido mi bolso.   *I've lost* my bag.

Date prisa. Vamos a *perder* el tren.   Hurry up! We're going *to miss* the train.

Demasiado tarde, ya *lo hemos perdido*. Ahora tenemos que esperar al siguiente.   Too late, *we've missed it*. Now we'll have to wait for the next one.

Llegué tarde a casa así que *me perdí* mi programa favorito.   I arrived home late and *missed* my favourite programme.

Perderse is used for *missing* something relating to your own routine or liking, or even for *losing* something, or for something or someone *getting lost*:

Me he perdido en la ciudad.   *I got lost* in the town.

Fallar means *to miss the target/mark, not to hit.*

Este sistema nunca *me ha fallado*.   This system has never *let me down/never failed me/has never missed.*

El cazador apuntó, disparó pero *falló* el blanco.   The hunter took aim, fired but *missed*.

Also useful to know

1   'To be missing' can be translated in two ways in Spanish:

Completa las frases con las palabras que *faltan*.   Complete the phrases with the *missing* words.

¿Has oído la noticia? Han encontrado a esa chica *desaparecida*.   Have you heard the news? They've found that *missing* girl.

2   Other translations of 'to miss':

No entendí todo lo que contaba.   *I missed/didn't catch* all of what was said.

Como llegué tarde a la estación, no *encontré* a mi novio.   As I arrived late at the station, I *missed* my boyfriend (who was waiting for me).

No dejes de ir a Harrods cuando estés en Londres.   *Don't miss* Harrods when in London.

3   **Faltar a clase.**   To miss a class.

4   **Fallar** can also mean 'to fail'.

Gastar, pasar – *to spend*

Gastar is used to *spend time, money, effort.*

Gasto todo mi dinero en ropa, revistas y maquillaje.   *I spend* all my money on clothes, magazines and make-up.

Gasta todo su tiempo en cuidar a los demás.   *She spends* all her time caring for others.

Mi coche *gasta* poca gasolina.   My car does not *use* much petrol (implication = not much money spent).

Pasar is used when *spending time.*

Pasé el fin de semana con mi novio.   *I spent* the weekend with my boyfriend.

¿Lo *pasaste* bien?   Did you *have a good time* (was it time *well spent*)?

Also useful to know

1   When **gastar** is used negatively it means 'to waste':
    Gastar tiempo.   *To waste* time.
    Gastar palabras.   *To waste* one's breath.

2   **Pasar** can also mean 'to pass an object to someone', 'to pass on an illness', 'to cross over', 'to excel/beat' or 'to suffer/go through'.

3   **Pasar** is also used in colloquial phrases:
    ¿Qué *pasa*?   What's *happening*?/What's *going on*?
    Siempre pasa igual/lo mismo.   Always the same old story.
    A veces *pasa* que . . .   It sometimes *happens* that . . .
    Paso.   *Count me out.* (Also used at cards.)

4   The word **pasota**, derived from *pasar*, refers to a person who could *not care less*/who lets everything *pass them by.*

Gustar, querer, tener cariño, encantar, interesar, parecer – *to (be) like*

Gustar means *to be pleasing to the person speaking* and is most often used in the third person singular or plural depending on the number of pleasing things.

Me gusta el chocolate blanco.   *I like* white chocolate.

Me gustan las flores con colores vivos.   *I like* flowers with bright colours.

Me gustas mucho con el pelo recogido.   *I like you* with your hair tied up.

Querer is used for *to like, to love* and *to want.*

Le *quieren* mucho en el trabajo.   He is well *liked* at work.

¿*Quieres* un café?   *Would you like* a coffee?

Te quiero mucho, mi amor.   *I love you* so much, darling.

Lo hizo *sin querer.*   He *didn't mean/want to* do it.

Como *quieras.*   As *you wish/want.*

Tener cariño is used when *liking/being fond of someone.*

Te tengo mucho cariño así que no me engañes.   *I'm very fond of you* so don't let me down.

Le tienes cariño ¿verdad?   *You like him,* don't you?

Encantar is used for liking something or someone but is a lot more expressive than gustar.

Me encantan las flores que me regalaste.   *I love* the flowers that you gave me.

Me encanta montar a caballo.   *I really like/love* to go horse-riding.

Ese actor *me encanta.*   *I really like/love/am a big fan of* that actor.

Interesar is used when the idea of *liking is expressed as an initial interest* with the possibility of finding out more.

¿*Te interesa* el fútbol?   *Do you like/are you interested in* football?

Ese asunto en las noticias *me interesa* mucho.   *I am very interested* in that news item (I would like to know more).

¿*Te interesa* salir conmigo este sábado?   *Would you like* to go out with me on Saturday? (Does the idea interest you?).

Parecer *is used when likening something/someone to something/someone else and for to look like/to seem.*

Pareces a una princesa en tu vestido tan bonito.   *You look like* a princess in such a pretty dress.

Parece a un niño cuando actúa así.   *He is like* a child when he acts this way.

Se parecen mucho.   *They look* very much *alike.*

Also useful to know

1   **Gustar** can also mean 'to taste'.

2   The words **cariño** and **cariñoso** mean 'darling/loved one' and 'affectionate'.

3   **Parecer**, when used as an impersonal verb, also has the colloquial meanings of 'to think/be of the opinion': *Me parece que sí* 'I think so/It seems like it to me'.

Ir, salir, funcionar, marchar – *to go*

Ir is used with a very general sense of *going* and usually when some form of movement is involved.

Ir a París.   *To go* to Paris.

Ir en coche.   *To go* by car.

Voy a ver.   *I'll go* and see.

¿Qué tal te *va*?   How's *it going*?

Salir is more often used to indicate *going out* rather than just simply *going*.

¿A qué hora *sale* el tren? When does the train *go/leave*?

Sale con un chico del barrio. She is *going (out)* with a local boy.

Funcionar/marchar are used to describe how something, usually mechanical, *goes*, *works* or *functions*.

El coche no *marcha*.   The car won't *go*.

Funciona con gasolina.   *It goes* on petrol.

Also useful to know

1   **Ir** has many idiomatic uses of its own in set phrases all with their own specific meanings (see page 91).

2   **Salir** can also mean 'to leave'.

3   Mi dinero *se gastó*.   All my money has *gone/been spent*.

4   ¡Cómo *pasa* el tiempo!   How time *goes/flies*!

5   *Se acabó* el tiempo.   Time *is up.*

6   **A la una, a las dos, a las tres.**   Going, going, gone!

Jugar, tocar, actuar – *to play*

Jugar is used for playing games, sports, gambling and when amusement is involved.

Juego bien al ajedrez.   I *play* chess well.

Cuando España *jugó* contra el Portugal, lo vi en la tele.   When Spain *played* (against) Portugal, I watched it on the telly.

El niño *juega* mucho con su ordenador.   The boy *plays* a lot on his computer.

¿Por qué no sales a *jugar*?   Why don't you go out *to play*?

Tocar is usually used when musical instruments are *being played.*

Tocan el violín y el saxofón.   *They play* the violin and the saxophone.

Tocar la retirada.   *To sound* the retreat.

Tocan a misa.   They are *ringing the bell* for Mass.

Actuar is used for *playing a part in/for* something.

Mi nieto *actúa* en una obra de teatro.   My grandson is *playing* (has a part in) in a theatre production.

Also useful to know

1   **Juguetear**, which stems from *jugar*, has a slightly more derivative meaning of 'to play around with' or 'to fiddle with'.

2   **Tocar** can also mean 'to touch'.

3   English can throw up a few problems with the verb 'to play' and, in these cases, it is important to examine the true meaning of the action being described before a correct translation can be reached. For example:
To *play up* (child).   *Dar guerra.*

To *play along.*   *Seguir el juego/dejarse llevar por la corriente.*
To *play* someone *along.*   *Dar largas* a alguien.
To *play on* someone's nerves.   *Atacar* los nervios a alguien.
To *play* a trick.   *Gastar* una broma.
To *play for* time.   *Tratar de ganar* tiempo.
What are you *playing at*?   Pero, *¿qué haces?*

Luchar, combatir, pelear, pugnar – *to fight*

Luchar – *to fight/struggle/wrestle.* This can be used both in a literal and a figurative sense:
Siempre *está luchando* por sus ideales.   *He's* always *fighting* for what he believes in.
Los dos chicos empezaron a *luchar* en la calle.   The two boys began *to fight* in the street.
¡*No luches* con eso, pide ayuda!   *Don't struggle* with that, ask for help.

Linked words:
La lucha.   Fight/struggle.
La lucha de las clases.   The class struggle.
La lucha contra la droga.   The fight/war against drugs.
La lucha libre.   Wrestling.
Luchador/a.   Combative or fighter/wrestler.

Combatir – *to fight/combat/attack.* The likeness of this word to the English *combat* does give a much stronger sense of military fighting and, indeed, the idea of not only fighting some sort of enemy but actually defeating them too.
Linked words:
El combate.   Fight/combat/contest (boxing)/struggle.
Estar fuera de combate.   To be out of action (not able to fight)/knocked out.
El combatiente.   Combatant.
La combatividad.   Fighting spirit/aggressiveness.
Combativo/a.   Full of fight/spirited/militant.

Pelear – *to fight/struggle, to scuffle/brawl, to quarrel/fall out.* I feel that the *fight* going on here is not always quite as physical or even morally charged as the above two verbs. Indeed, **pelear** can be merely with words with neither fisticuffs nor instruments needed!

¡Deja de *pelear* con tu hermano!   Stop *arguing/squabbling* with your brother!

Los niños siempre *pelean* en la guardería.   The children are always *falling out* at the nursery.

Linked words:

La pelea.   Fight/tussle/quarrel/row.

Armar una pelea.   To kick up a fuss/row.

Una pelea de gallos.   Cockfight.

Un gallo de pelea.   Fighting cock.

Peleador/a.   Quarrelsome.

Estar peleado/a con alguien.   To be on bad terms with someone.

Peleón/a.   Pugnacious/aggressive.

Pugnar – *to fight/struggle/strive for*. This verb initially sounds as if it is the more morally backed of the four but it is interesting to note that many of its linked words actually refer to the world of boxing:

La pugna.   Struggle/conflict.

Entrar/estar en pugna con.   To clash with.

Un púgil.   Boxer.

El pugilato.   Boxing/conflict.

El pugilismo.   Boxing.

El/la pugilista.   Boxer.

Pugilístico (adj).   Boxing.

Also useful to know

1 **Peleón** when used to describe a wine means 'cheap/ordinary'.

2 Other words which can be used when the 'fight' is purely verbal are **disputa/disgusto**.

3 In the sense of 'fighting back' the verb to use is **defenderse**.

4 When considering a figurative use of 'fight' the word is **ánimo**:

Ya no le queda *ánimo*.   There's no *fight* left in him.

5 Other useful phrases:

Luchar en vano. To *fight* a losing battle.

Abrirse paso por la multitud. To *fight* one's way through a crowd.

Negar una acusación. To *fight* a (legal) case.

6 To fight off – *repeler/rechazar* (attacker), *reprimir* (urge), *sacudirse* (sleep/illness).

Morir, fallecer, fenecer – *to die*

Morir – the most used translation of *to die* but it can also mean *to die down/out* (of fire/light), *to come to an end*, *to come out at*:

El mendigo *murió de hambre.* The beggar *died from hunger/starved to death.*

Al *morir* el día. As the day *ends* /As night *falls.* (Quite a poetic usage.)

Esta calle *muere* en la playa. This road *ends* at the beach. (More common to use *termina/acaba/sale.*)

Linked words:

La muerte. Death.

Muerto/a. Dead/lifeless.

Moribundo. Dying/a dying person.

Fallecer – *to die/pass away.* This verb is used in a similar way as in English with an almost euphemistic sense in order to soften the blow:

'*Ha fallecido* tu padre (your father *has passed away*)' will never be quite as harsh as '*ha muerto* tu padre (your father *has died*)'.

Linked words:

El fallecimiento. Decease/death.

Fallecido/a. Deceased/late.

Fenecer – *to come to an end/cease* and really only used euphemistically to mean *to pass away/die.*

Also useful to know

Morir, when used reflexively, makes the death much more of a personal issue:

Se me murió mi perro. My dog *died* (and I'm really feeling it).

It also has a string of figurative uses:

¡Me muero de hambre!   I'm starving!

¡Me moría de risa!   I just couldn't stop laughing!

Se muere por su novio.   *She's mad about* her boyfriend.

¡Me muero por verte!   *I'm dying* to see you!

Note the phrase **en su agonía**, meaning 'dying breath', 'on his/her deathbed', 'in his/her dying moments' (see page 66).

Necesitar, hacer falta, requerir – *to need, require*

Necesitar means *to need, want, be required.*

Todos *necesitamos* amigos.   *We* all *need* friends.

Se necesita niñera.   Baby-sitter *wanted/required.*

Hacer falta is used when something *which is missing is needed.*

Me hace falta bronceador para ir de vacaciones a la playa.   *I need* suntan lotion for my holiday at the beach.

Me hacen falta unos zapatos nuevos para ir a la boda.

I need some new shoes to go to the wedding.

Hace falta que venga la policía.   The police are *needed.*

Requerir is used when something is needed/required as a prerequisite.

Todo trabajo bien hecho *requiere* dedicación.   All good work *requires* dedication.

El juez *requirió* a los testigos.   The judge *sent for* (required the presence of) the witnesses.

Also useful to know

1   Remember that **hacer falta** is an impersonal verb. As you can see in the examples above, the subject of the verb in Spanish is the object of the verb in English.

2   **Faltar** on its own means 'to be lacking or missing' and is always used in the third person.

3   **Falta** is often commonly mistaken to mean 'fault'.

4   **No faltaba más/No faltaría más** are extremely courteous way of saying 'Don't mention it'.

5   **¡Lo que me faltaba!**   That's all I needed!

Poner, colocar, meter – *to put*

Poner means *to put/ place/put on (clothes).*
¿Qué me *pongo* para la fiesta?   What *shall I put on/wear*
for the party?
Pónlo en su sitio.   *Put it back* (in its place)/(where you
found it).
Poner algo aparte.   *To put* something aside/on one side.

Colocar means *to place/put/position/arrange* something/
someone. It is much more precise than *poner.*
Colócate cerca de la ventana.   *Sit (put)* yourself next to
the window.
A mi madre le gusta mucho *colocar* las cosas bien en su
sitio.   My mother loves *to arrange* things properly in
their place.

Meter means *to put* but is usually followed by '*in/on*'.
No *te metas* en mis asuntos.   *Mind* your own business
(don't put yourself in my business).
Meter dinero en el banco.   *To put* money in the bank.
Meter miedo a alguien.   *To scare* (put the frighteners on)
someone.

Also useful to know

1   **Poner** can also be used for 'to show (films)', 'to install
    version (something)' and to lay (eggs)'!

2   **Meter** can also mean 'to score a goal'.

3   Both **poner** and **meter** are used in idiomatic phrases:
    Ponérsele a uno la carne de gallina   To get goose
    pimples.
    Poner los puntos sobre los íes   To dot the i's and cross
    the t's.
    Meter la pata.   To put your foot in it.
    Meter las narices.   To poke your nose in.
    (see page 92).

Probar, intentar, tratar de, ensayar, cansar – *to try*

Probar is the verb most often used to mean *to try (of food or drink)/sample* or *to try something/someone out*:
¿Qué opinas si *le probamos* para el puesto?   What do you think of *giving him a try* for the job?
Prueba la tortilla, ¡está deliciosa!   *Try* the omelette, it's delicious!
¿*Nunca has probado* la sangría? ¡No me lo creo!   *You've never tried/tasted* sangria? I can't believe it!
Si te gusta tanto la falda, ¿por qué no te *la pruebas*?   If you like the skirt so much, why don't you *try it on*?

Intentar is probably one of the most commonly used verbs for *to try/attempt something* (note its similarity with the English idea of intention):
¡Venga, *inténtalo*!   Go on, *have a go/try it!*
Vale la pena *intentarlo*.   It's worth *a try.*

Tratar de, again with a similarity to the English, is used to mean *to try/endeavour to* and is usually followed by a direct infinitive:
Tratar de hacer algo.   *To try to* do something.
Cuando venga tu abuelita, *trata de* ser amable.   *Try to* be nice when your granny arrives.

Ensayar has a slightly different meaning of 'try' which is *to try out/test* or, in the theatrical world, *to rehearse*:
Ensayar a hacer algo.   *To practise* doing something.
Está ensayando para su papel en la obra navideña de la escuela.   *She is rehearsing* for her role/part in the school Christmas play.
Lo estamos ensayando para ver si funciona.   *We're trying it out* to see if it works.

Cansar is not often used with the primary idea of trying, as in making an attempt of some description, but rather with the idea of *being trying* and therefore causing the primary meaning of cansar which is *to tire out*:

Utilizar mucho la computadora *cansa* mucho los ojos. Over-using the computer can be very *trying/taxing/straining/ tiring* on the eyes.

Cuando hay mucho jaleo por poca cosa, *me cansa muchísimo.*   When there is a lot of fuss over nothing, *it is very trying/it wears me down.*

Also useful to know

1   **Probar** can also mean 'to prove/show/demonstrate' and, in certain situations, 'to suit/agree with':
    No me prueba bien el café tan fuerte.   Such strong coffee *does not agree with me.*

2   A linked word with *probar* is **probeta,** which is a 'test tube', and thus **niño probeta** is a 'test-tube baby'.

3   **Tratar de** can also mean 'to be about/deal with/talk about/discuss':
    Bodas de Sangre, la famosa obra de Lorca, *trata de* la vida de pueblo, sus familias y sus creencias.   *Blood Wedding*, the famous Lorca play *is about* village life, its families and their beliefs.

4   A different preposition after **tratar** can change its meaning: *tratar a/tratar con* means 'to have dealings with/to treat (someone)'. Note also that the reflexive usage in a very common phrase – **se trata de** – means 'to be about/ to be a question of':
    ¿De qué se *trata?*   What is it *about?/What's the trouble?/What's up?*

5   **Ensayar** can also mean 'to assay' (of metals), meaning to subject the metal to some form of chemical analysis. **Un ensayo** is also used for 'a try' in rugby terminology.

6   Other phrases where the idea of 'trying' is more apparent in the English are:
    Poner todo su empeño/hacer todo lo posible.   To try one's best/hardest.
    Abusar de la paciencia de alguien.   To try someone's patience.

Poner a prueba.   To try/put to the test.

Procesar/enjuiciar a alguien.   to try someone (in a court of law).

Querer, necesitar, desear, esperar – *to want*

Querer/necesitar these two verbs have already been discussed in previous sections (see pages 13 and 20 respectively).

Desear means *to want/desire/wish for/look forward to*. The implication with this verb is a positive one with very strong overtones.

Estoy deseando ver a mi abuela después de tantos años.   *I am looking forward to* seeing (really want to see) my grandmother after all these years.

Te *deseo* suerte.   *I wish* you luck.

Estoy deseando que termine ya.   *I am longing for* (really want) this to finish.

Deja mucho que *desear*.   It leaves a lot *to be desired*.

Esperar is used when what is wanted is *hoped/wished/waited for* and with an element of not knowing if it will actually happen.

Espero que tengas suerte en los exámenes.   (*I hope you have*) good luck in your exams.

Espero que llegue pronto.   *I hope* she gets here soon.

¡*Espera* un momento!   *Wait/Just* a minute!

¿*Espera* visita?   *Are you expecting* someone?

Also useful to know

At this point I feel it necessary to point out that many of the verbs in the last four sections may have sexual connotations in a more colloquial setting, particularly in a spoken context (see chapter 6 page 99).

Saber, conocer, reconocer, informarse, enterarse – *to know*

Saber is used for knowledge of facts, dates and how to do things.

Sé conducir.   I *know how* to drive.

Sabe muchas cosas.   He/she *knows* a lot of things.

¿*Sabes* cuándo llega?   *Do you know* when he/she will arrive?

Hoy es mi cumpleaños. Lo *sé*.   Today is my birthday I *know*.

Saber la diferencia.   *To know* the difference.

Conocer is used for knowledge of people and places.

Conozco a esa persona.   I *know* that person.

¿*Conoces* a ese chico guapo?   *Do you know* that good-looking boy?

He vivido muchos años en Altea. ¿De verdad? No lo*conozco.*   I lived in Altea for many years. Really? I don't *know* it.

Reconocer is used when the speaker knows someone or something based upon previous information. (Idea of 'realising' or 'recognising'.)

La *reconocí* en seguida.   I *knew (recognised)* her at once.

Los ciegos *reconocen* a otros por la voz.   Blind people *know* others by their voice.

Reconozco que tienes razón.   I *realise/know* that you're right.

Enterarse/informarse are used for finding out about things when the speaker has no previous knowledge of them.

Quiero *enterarme* de lo que pasó.   I want *to know* what happened.

¿*Te has enterado* de lo de María?   *Did you know* about María?

Para que *te enteres.* (fam.)   Just so that *you know.*

Also useful to know

1   **Saber** can also means 'to taste of'.

2   **¿Sabes?** ('You know') is often tagged on to the end of phrases where some information has been given:

   No es fácil ¿*sabes*?   It's not easy, *you know.*

3   **Que yo *sepa*** ('as far as *I know*'). Subjunctive use of **saber** to portray possible doubt (see page 132).

4 Ser un *sabelotodo.*   To be a *know-all.*

5 Estar *enterado.*   To be *in the know.*

6 **¡Fíjate!** is used for the exclamation 'Imagine that!/Well, what do you know!'.

7 The infamous phrase 'We'll let you know' is **Te avisaremos**.

Ser, estar, haber – *to be*

In the quest for fluency, the thorn in the side of most non-native speakers of Spanish is 'which verb do I need?'
A very basic rule of thumb is this:

Ser is used in the following situations: condition (what/who someone is, job, nationality), possession, permanent characteristics (colour, size, shape, character, where from), number, time/events and before nouns.
Estar is used for: location/position, health, temporary situations/characteristics (sad, cold, tired), dates and to form continuous tenses and certain idioms and phrases.
Haber means 'to be' when used in compound tenses in the form of an auxiliary verb. Note also use of *hay* (there is/are).

Also useful to know

1 Some adjectives differ in meaning whether they take *ser* or *estar*. When **estar** is used with an adjective which would normally take **ser**, the meaning becomes 'to look/appear':
¡Qué guapa *estás*!   How pretty *you look* (today).
Note also the different meanings that adjectives take when used with *ser* or *estar* respectively[1]:

aburrido   boring/bored
bueno   good/tasty
cansado   tiring/tired
despierto   alert/awake
interesado   self-seeking/interested
listo   clever/ready

---

[1] List reproduced from Phil Turk and Mike Zollo, *¡Acción Gramática!: New Advanced Spanish Grammar* (Hodder Arnold 2006.)

> *malo*   bad/ill
> *rico*   rich/delicious
> *seguro*   safe/convinced
> *verde*   smutty/unripe/green (not ripe enough)
> *vivo*   alert/alive

2   Although *ser* is used for states/conditions of a more permanent nature, note that **ser** usually goes with the following adjectives: *pobre, feliz, desgraciado, inocente, culpable* and *consciente*.

3   A good rule of thumb: if there is not a good reason to use *estar*, use *ser*. This is a useful guide but it is not foolproof!

4   Many idioms take *ser* or *estar* despite all the above rules (see chapter 5 page 89).

5   **Tener** is also used when describing emotional and physical conditions:
Tengo hambre.   *I am* hungry.
Tengo sueño.   *I am* tired.

6   **Hacer** is used to describe some weather conditions
Hace frío.   *It is* cold.
Hace viento.   *It is* windy.

Tener – *to have* is most commonly used for *to have* or *to own*.
Tengo los ojos azules.   *I have (got)* blue eyes.
Tengo el pelo rubio.   *I have (got)* fair hair.
En casa *tenemo*s tres perros y dos gatos.   At home *we have (got)* three dogs and two cats.
En mis sueños *tengo* un Porche dorado.   In my dreams *I have/own* a golden Porsche.
Tiene tres hermanos ¡pobrecita!   *She has* three brothers, poor thing!

Also useful to know

The verb 'to have' in English has many uses which each have their own individual translation in Spanish.

1 When used as an auxiliary verb in compound tenses, the verb used is **haber**:

Ha salido pero te *ha* dejado una nota.   He's gone out but *he's* left you a note.

2 When used as a tag question ('Have you?'), set expressions are more likely to be used:

Tengo dos hermanas gemelas. *¡No me digas!*   I have twin sisters. *Have you?/You don't say!*

Has dejado de fumar *¿verdad?*   You've stopped smoking, *haven't you?*

3 When talking about having something to eat or drink, **tomar** can be used.

4 Often it is the actual meaning of the phrase which will give the correct translation of 'to have':

Pasar una tarde agradable.   *To have/spend* a nice afternoon.

Dar una fiesta.   *To have/throw/give* a party.

5 Sometimes the verb itself becomes completely independent:

Pasear.   To have/go for a walk.

Nadar.   To have a swim/to swim.

6 There are also many idioms and expressions that use the verb **tener** but which have nothing to do with the verb 'to have':

Tener frío/calor/sed/hambre.   To be cold/hot/thirsty/hungry.

Tener ganas de.   To feel like.

Tener malas pulgas.   To be bad-tempered.

Tener inconveniente.   To mind/object to.

Tener palabra.   To keep one's word.

(see page 93)

Tomar, coger, llevar, sacar, cobrar – *to take*

Tomar/coger

These two verbs have already been discussed in previous sections (page 3).

Llevar means *to take, to carry, to wear, to lead to.*

¿Adónde me *llevas*?   Where are *you taking* me?

¿Qué *llevo* hoy para salir?   What shall *I wear* to go out today?

El botones me *llevó* la maleta.   The bellboy *carried/took* my suitcase.

Iré adónde el camino me *lleve.*   I will go wherever the road *leads/takes* me.

Sacar means *to take something/someone from somewhere else* so it is usually used to express *to take out/off.*

Hoy *he sacado* mil libras del banco.   Today *I took/drew* a thousand pounds *out* of the bank.

El sábado te voy a *sacar* a bailar.   I'm *taking* you *out* dancing on Saturday.

Sacarse la ropa.   *To take off* one's clothes (L. Am. usage).

Cobrar means *to take* (*money*) or when some form of cost is involved, whether emotional or financial.

Cobro a finales de mes.   *I get paid* (take my money) at the end of the month.

El accidente *cobró* 100 víctimas.   The accident *claimed/took the lives of* 100 victims.

Also useful to know

1 **Llevar,** when used reflexively, can mean 'to get/receive':
 Se llevó un susto cuando vio que el coche no paraba.   *He got* a shock when he saw that the car wasn't going to stop.
 El criado *se llevó* una buena paliza al no seguir las órdenes de su amo.   The servant *got/had* a good beating for not following his master's orders.

2 **Sacar** can also be used in certain set phrases:
 Sacar un pasaporte.   *To obtain* a passport.
 Sacar una foto.   *To take* a photo.
 Sacar una copia.   *To take* a copy.
 Sacar buenas/malas notas.   *To get* good/bad results.
 Sacar is also used for serving in tennis, kicking off in football and other ways of *starting* a sporting activity.

3 A curious thing about **cobrar** is that, despite the fact that it is a very common verb, there is no exact equivalent in English. Its meaning usually has something to do with *costing*:

Note: *Cobrar* el sueldo.   To *collect* one's salary.

Cobrar la factura.   To *collect* the money to be paid/for the invoice.

¿Cuánto va a *cobrar*?   How much are you going *to charge*?

¿Cuánto *cobra* por hora?   What is your hourly *charge/rate*?

Usar, emplear, utilizar, servirse de, aprovechar, agotar – *to use*

Usar is generally used to mean *to use*, *make use of* or *to wear or take* (clothes of a particular size):

Esto ya no *se usa*.   That is not *used/not in fashion* any more.

¿Qué talla *usas*?   What size *do you take*?

Emplear is the verb commonly used to mean *to use or employ something or someone* or *to spend, invest or occupy (time or money)*:

Emplear mal.   To *misuse*.

¿Cuántos *empleados* tienes?   How many *employees* do you have?

Para esto, hace falta *emplear* un martillo muy fuerte.   You need (*to use*) a big hammer for that.

Utilizar is the verb to use for making use of something, utilizing something:

En las obras de Lorca *se utilizan* muchos símbolos para los efectos teatrales.   In the works of Lorca many symbols *are made use of* for dramatic effect.

Servirse de, again, has the meaning of *to make use of* but also can mean *to put something to use* or even *to take advantage of*:

Se sirvió de su amistad con la directora.   *He took advantage/made use of* his friendship with the boss.

Aprovechar is used to mean *to make (good) use of, to exploit, to profit from, to make the most of*:

¡No *te aproveches de* mí!   Don't *take advantage of* me!

Aprovecha de tus vacaciones.   *Make the most of* your holidays.

Agotar is used when the main meaning is *to use up/exhaust/ finish/drain/empty/ tire out*:

Estoy agotado.   I'm *worn out.*

Los recursos están *agotados.*   The supplies are *dried up/ finished.*

Este libro *está agotado.*   This book *has sold out/is out of print.*

Also useful to know

1 **Soler hacer algo** means 'to be in the habit of doing something' 'used to doing something'.

2 **De usar y tirar** is one way of saying 'disposable'.

3 The phrase **¡Te está bien empleado!** is one way of saying 'It serves you right!'

4 When used with the reflexive form in the phrase **emplearse a fondo**, the meaning is 'to do one's utmost/best'.

5 Note the meaning of **¡Que aproveche!** to mean the equivalent of the French 'Bon appétit!' or the English 'Enjoy your meal!'

6 **Agotado** can also be used to describe a battery as being 'flat' or 'run down'.

Helping you learn

Progress checks

1 Looking at the English side only, translate a whole section of one item into Spanish and check your answers.
2 Try to listen to some Spanish (real conversation, tape, video, radio) until you spot one of the problem words/ phrases.
3 Write down explanations for differences between one set of verbs available in Spanish to translate one verb in English and check your answers.

Discussion points

1 Find out if your fellow students have difficulties with the same words/phrases/ structures.
2 Never miss an opportunity to ask a native Spanish speaker to explain differences which you have come across.
3 Do you agree that you never question oddity found in your mother tongue?

Study tips
1 Never wait until you can say everything in perfect Spanish. Start using the language straight away, even mixing it with English if you have to!
2 Speak in Spanish at any opportunity.

Choosing the right word - 1

This chapter aims to point out a few common errors but will be enlarged upon over the next couple of chapters too. The list has been divided up into the following sections for ease of reference : adjectives, nouns and connectors.

■ Adjectives : the right word for *brown, free, old, slim* and *wrong*

■ Nouns : the right word for *country, face, half, help, speed, time* and *work*

■ Connectors : the right word for *and, but, for, or* and *so*

Adjectives

Marrón, color café, castaño/a, moreno/a, bronceado/a, dorado/a, negro/a – *brown*

We can see just from the above list that the translation we choose all depends upon the *shade* of brown we wish to portray. After all, and in comparsion, how many shades of blue can you think of in English?

Marrón is only ever used in a singular or plural form and is the standard translation of just plain *brown*:
Tengo los ojos *marrones* y el pelo *castaño.*   I have *brown* eyes and *brown* hair.

Color café is a much lighter shade of brown, *coffee coloured,* and is usually used to refer to clothes, furniture and other items:

Me encanta ese abrigo *color café*.   I love that *coffee-coloured* coat.

Castaño/a is very useful! Usually used for physical descriptions of hair and eyes:
Tengo los ojos *castaños* y el pelo *castaño*.   I have *hazel* eyes and *light-brown* hair.
Compare the English possibilities here from *chestnut/hazel* shades through to varying shades of *light brown*.

Moreno/a, again, is usually used for the physical description of hair and eyes but can also refer to skin colour and be used to mean *dark* (as opposed to fair):
Tengo los ojos *morenos* y el pelo *moreno*.   I have *dark (brown)* eyes and hair.
Soy *moreno/a*.   I am *dark-skinned/dark-haired* (and possibly with *dark-brown* eyes too!).
Moreno/a can also be used to refer to *black* skin/hair when compared with those of a lighter shade.

Bronceado/a means *bronzed/tanned*, the inference being that the skin is not naturally that colour.

Dorado/a means *golden* and can refer to skin colour but is also used for the culinary term *browned/golden*.

Negro/a primarily means *black* but can also be used to mean *very tanned/too tanned* or *very dark brown* (eyes).

Libre, suelto, liberal, gratuito, gratis, independiente – *free*

Libre generally means *free from something, unoccupied, vacant, spare*:
¿Estás *libre*?   Are you *free*?
¿Está *libre* este asiento?   Is this seat *free*?
Al aire *libre*.   In the *open* air.
Ir por *libre*.   To go it *alone*.
Un tiro *libre*.   A *free* kick.

Suelto means *free from previous problems, imprisonment, ties*; it has the idea of *loose*:
Dinero *suelto*.   *Loose* change.

El ladrón anda *suelto*.   The thief is *on the loose/walking free*.

Llevar el pelo *suelto*.   To wear one's hair *loose*.

The word *soltura*, which comes from *suelto*, means *looseness/ fluency*:

Hablas español *con soltura*.   You speak Spanish *fluently*.

Liberal means *free* as in *open, generous*:

Tener la mente *liberal* frente a los problemas.   To have an *open mind* when faced with problems.

No me gustan sus ideas tan *liberales*.   I don't like her *open-minded/outspoken* ideas.

Gratuito means *free* when something is *gratuitous* or *uncalled for*:

Un permiso para entrada *gratuita*.   *Free* pass.

No hagas comentarios *gratuitos*.   Don't make *uncalled- for* comments.

Gratis means *free/no charge*

Obtener algo *gratis*.   To get something *for free*.

¿Cuánto pagaste por la entrada? Nada, entré *gratis*.   How much did it cost you to get in? Nothing, I got in *(for) free*.

Independiente means *free from others*:

Hacerse *independiente*.   To become *independent*.

Un piso *independiente*.   *Self-contained* flat.

Una persona *independiente*.   *Free* agent.

Also useful to know

Un regalo obsequio.   Free gift.

Un puerto franco.   Free port.

La libertad de expresión.   Free(dom of) speech.

El libre cambio.   Free trade.

El libre albedrío.   Free will.

Viejo/a, antiguo/a, anciano/a – *old*

Viejo/a is probably the main word we learn to mean *old*:

La ropa *vieja*.   *Old/second-hand* clothing.

Hacerse/ponerse viejo/a.   To get/grow old.

Los viejos.   *The old* or more familiarly *my old folks* (parents).

Mi viejo/a (L. Am.).   My old man/woman (partner).

Linked words:

Un/a viejito/a.   An old person/friend (L. Am.).

Envejecer.   To age, to make/grow/look/seem old.

Envejecido/a.   Old/aged/old-looking.

Después de estar tan enfermo, *ha envejecido* mucho.

After being so ill, *he has aged* terribly.

La vejez.   Old age.

Antiguo/a is the idea of *old* but with a tendency towards *ancient/former/ex-/senior*:

Soy *antigua* alumna.   I am an *ex*-pupil.

A la antigua.   In the *old-fashioned* way.

En lo antiguo.   In the *olden* days/*ancient* times.

Es el abogado *más antiguo*.   He is the *senior* lawyer.

Los antiguos.   The ancients.

Linked words:

La antigualla.   Old thing/relic/old story/has-been.

Las antiguallas.   Old things/junk.

Antiguamente.   Formerly/once/long ago/in ancient times.

Una/la antigüedad.   Antiquity/age/seniority/antique.

Una tienda de antigüedades.   An antiques shop.

Anciano/a, when used as an adjective, means *old/aged*, but can be used as a noun to mean an *old man/woman* or, in a religious context, an *elder*:

La ancianidad.   Old age.

Also useful to know

Antaño.   In days of old.

Mi hija tiene 9 años.   My daughter is 9 years old.

Una patraña/un cuento de viejas.   An old wives' tale.

Más viejo que Matusalén.   As old as the hills.

Una solterona.   An old maid.

Una residencia/asilo de ancianos.   An old people's home.

El Antiguo Testamento.   The Old Testament.

Sirve cualquier cosa.   Any old thing will do.

El subsidio de vejez/ la jubilación.   Old-age pension.

Un/a pensionista/jubilado/a.   Old-age pensioner.

Anticuado/a.   Old-fashioned.

Mi hermano mayor.   My older brother.

Un viejo verde.   A dirty old man.

Delgado/a, esbelto/a, flaco/a – *slim*

Delgado/a is the commonest translation for *thin/slim*:

Me gustaría estar *más delgada.*   I would like to be *slimmer.*

However, it can also be used to mean *delicate/tenuous/sharp/ clever.*

Linked words:

La delgadez.   Thinness/slimness/delicateness/ tenuousness/sharpness.

Adelgazar.   To make slim/slender, to lose (weight)/slim, to pare/whittle/sharpen.

Adelgazador (adj).   Slimming.

El adelgazamiento (noun).   Slimming.

Esbelto/a is used when *slim* can also mean *slender/svelte/ graceful*:

Tiene la nuca *esbelta* como un cisne.   She has a swan-like neck (long and *slender*).

Flaco/a is not as complimentary as the first two: it does mean *slim* but with a tendency towards *thin/skinny*:

Ponerse flaco (L. Am.). To get *thin* (and not necessarily for the better).

Flaco/a can also mean *weak/feeble*:

Su punto flaco.   His *weak point/weakness.*

Después del accidente tiene *la memoria flaca.*   Since the accident her *memory has been bad/short.*

Linked words:

La flacura.   Thinness/skinniness.

El flaco.   Weak spot/failing.

Also useful to know

Sus posibilidades son bastante *limitadas.*   His chances are pretty *slim.*

Estoy a/haciendo régimen.   I'm *slimming* (on a diet).

Los recursos son *escasos* en el Tercer Mundo.   Resources are *thin* in the Third World (not in abundance).

Está en los huesos.   He is very *thin/skin and bone/as thin as a rake.*

Esfumarse.   To vanish into *thin air.*

Se le agotaba la paciencia a la madre.   The mother's patience was *wearing thin.*

En las montañas más altas del mundo, el aire está más *enrarecido.*   In the highest mountains of the world, the air is at its *thinnest.*

Una excusa apenas *disimulada*   a *thinly-veiled* excuse.

Cortado en trozos *finos*   cut into *thin* slices/*thinly* sliced.

Es un país *poco poblado.*   It is a *thinly-populated* country.

Malo, no tener razón, equivocarse/estar equivocado, incorrecto, inexacto, no adecuado/apropiado, impropio – *wrong*

There is no one Spanish word that covers all the meanings of the English word *wrong.*

When *wrong* means 'morally or ethically wrong', the word used is **malo**:

Has hecho algo muy *malo.*   You have done something very *wrong.*

¿Qué hay de *malo* en esto?   What's *wrong* in that?

When *wrong* means 'incorrect', there are several possibilities in Spanish and not all of them are interchangeable:

– When people are involved, **no tener razón**, **equivocarse** or **estar equivocado** are used:

No tienes razón.   You are *wrong/mistaken.*

Lo siento pero has marcado un número *equivocado.*   I'm sorry but you have dialled a *wrong* number.

Se ha equivocado Usted de autobús.   You have got on the *wrong* bus.

– When talking about 'wrong' information, answers and so on, **incorrecto**, **inexacto**, **equivocado or mal** are used:

El alumno contestó *mal* en la prueba.   The pupil answered *wrongly* in the test.

Has escrito *mal* mi nombre.   You have written my name *wrongly*.

Esta información está *equivocada*.   This information is *wrong*.

La cuenta es *incorrecta/inexacta*.   The bill is *wrong*.

– When *wrong* means 'inappropriate or unwanted', **no adecuado/apropiado** or **impropio** are used:

No es el momento *apropiado/adecuado* para discutir estas cosas.   It is the *wrong* time to discuss these things.

Siempre dices algo *impropio* cuando estás frente a mis padres.   You always say the *wrong* thing to my parents.

– When *wrong* expresses an undesired outcome, it can have a variety of translations:

No es la revista que *hacía falta*.   It's the *wrong* magazine (not the one requested).

Nos hemos *equivocado* de andén.   We're on the *wrong* platform.

¿Por qué llevas tu camiseta *al revés*?   Why are you wearing your t-shirt the *wrong way* out? (inside out).

Está claro que mi trabajo *no me conviene*.   It's obvious that I'm in the *wrong* job.

Los libros están *mal* colocados en la estantería.   The books are in the *wrong* place on the shelf.

Al empezar a practicar la flauta, tocarás mucha *nota falsa*.   On learning to play the flute, you'll hit/play many a *wrong* note.

¿Por qué conducen los ingleses por el lado *contrario* de la calle?   Why do the English drive on the *wrong* side of the road?

– When *wrong* means 'amiss', 'to have something wrong', the verb *pasar* is used:

¿Qué te *pasa*, cariño?   What's *wrong*, my love?

¿Qué *pasa* aquí?   What's *wrong*/going on here?

Le *pasa* algo a mi coche porque no anda.   Something is *wrong* with my car because it won't go.

Also useful to know

Distinguir entre el bien y el mal.   To tell right from *wrong.*
Entiéndeme bien.   Don't get me *wrong.*
Todo salió mal.   Everything went *wrong.*
Hiciste mal en hacerle caso.   You were *wrong* to listen to him.

Nouns

Campo, país, patria, nación – *country*

These words can all be used to refer to the word *country* but their focus, once again, is very individual.

Campo is used for *country* when referring specifically to the *countryside*:
Vamos al *campo* este fin de semana.   Let's go out into the *country(side)* this weekend.
¿Dónde prefieres vivir: en la ciudad o en *el campo*?   Where do you prefer to live: in the town or out in the *country(side)*?

País is used for *country* in a geographical sense:
¿De qué *país* vienes?   Which *country* are you from?
En la gran reunión, había representantes de todos los *países* del mundo.   There were representatives from all over the world (from all the *countries* in the world) at the big meeting.

Patria is used for *country* when referring to *native land/ homeland*:
El ejército defiende a su *patria* en tiempos de guerra.   The army defends its *country* in times of war.
Por dondequiera que vaya, Inglaterra siempre será mi *patria*.   Wherever I go, England will always be my *country (homeland)*.

Nación is used for *country* when referring more to *nation/ nationality*:
Las *Naciones* Unidas.   The United *Nations*.

Cara, rostro, semblante – *face*

Cara is the word we all know and love to mean *face* and, apart from the physical aspect of its primary meaning, *cara* is used in many an idiomatic phrase where the meaning can be quite different!

A cara descubierta.   Openly.

De cara al oeste.   Facing west.

Cara al futuro.   With a view to the future/looking towards the future.

Mirar a alguien a la cara.   To look someone in the face/in the eye.

Asomar la cara.   To show one's face.

Dar la cara.   To face the consequences.

Dar/hacer cara a.   To face up to.

Dar la cara por otro.   To answer for somebody else.

Decir algo en/por la cara de alguien.   To say something to someone's face.

Echar algo en cara.   To reproach.

Hacer a dos caras.   To engage in double-dealing.

Plantar cara a.   To confront.

Romper la cara a alguien.   To smash someone's face in.

Sacar la cara por alguien.   To stick up for someone.

Tener buena cara.   To look good.

No volver la cara atrás.   Not to flinch.

Cara also has three other important meanings:

– *look/appearance* and usually preceded by the verb *tener/poner*:

Tener cara de alegría.   To have a cheerful expression.

Tener cara de pocos amigos.   To look miserable/have a long face.

Tener cara de monja boba.   To look all innocent.

Poner cara de circunstancias.   To look resigned.

Poner mala cara.   To pull a face.

Poner cara de vinagre.   To be sour-faced.

– *cheek/nerve*, again, often used with *tener*:

¡Qué cara tienes!   You've got some nerve/cheek!

Es un cara dura.   He has got some nerve!

Tener más cara que espalda/que un elefante con paperas.   To have the gall to do something/an incredible nerve/unbelievable cheek.

– *face/side* (of a coin, for example)
Cara o cruz.   Heads or tails.

Rostro is also used for *face* but is closer in meaning to the English word *countenance* and so takes into consideration a *mood or expression*:
Se le veía en el rostro.   You could tell (how she was feeling) by the look on her *face*.

Semblante is used for *face/look/composure*:
Componer el semblante.   To regain one's composure.
Alterar el semblante a alguien.   To upset someone.
Semblantear (L. Am.).   To look straight in the face.

Also useful to know

Hasta hartarte.   Until you are blue *in the face.*
Ha desaparecido de *la faz* de la tierra.   It has vanished off *the face* of the earth.
Hacer muecas.   To make/pull *faces.*
A primera vista.   On the *face* of it.
Poner al mal tiempo buena cara.   To put a *brave face* on.
Desprestigiarse/perder prestigio.   To *lose face.*
Salvar las apariencias.   To *save face.*
Estar enfrente de.   To be opposite/*facing.*
Dar a/tener vistas a.   To be overlooking.
Enfrentarse con/afrontar/hacer frente a/soportar.   To *face up to*/confront.
Afrontar las consecuencias.   To *face* the music.
¡Seamos realistas!   *Let's face* it!
Una mascarilla.   A *face pack.*
Una manopla.   A *facecloth*/flannel.
Creerse algo a pie juntillas.   To take something at *face value.*

Medio vs mitad – *half*

Both these words mean *half* but each has its own specific uses.

Medio is usually used as an adjective and therefore has to agree in quantity and gender with the noun it modifies:
Estaré en tu casa dentro de *media* hora.   I will be at your house in the next *half hour/half an hour*.
Voy a necesitar otra *media* docena de huevos para las tortillas.   I am going to need another *half* a dozen eggs for the omelettes.

Medio can also be used adverbially.
Si me levanto demasiado pronto por la mañana, me encuentro *medio* dormida.   If I get up too early in the mornings, I find that I am still *half* asleep!

Mitad, on the other hand, is a feminine noun:
Hacia la *mitad* del cuento, el niño se durmió.   *Halfway* through the story, the little boy fell asleep.
Me queda *la mitad*.   I only have *half* left.
A *mitad* de precio.   *Half* price.
En *mitad* de la calle.   In the *middle* of the street.

Ayuda, socorro, auxilio – *help*

Ayuda is most commonly used for *help/assistance/aid*:
Ayúdame a levantar esto, por favor.   *Help me* to lift this, please.
La *ayuda* humanitaria.   Humanitarian *aid*.
Linked words:
El/la ayudante/a.   Helper/assistant/technician.
Ayudar.   To help/assist/aid.
Note: in medical terms, *una ayuda* is the word for an *enema* and, in Latin America, the word for *a laxative* (the idea of helping/assisting should be fairly self-explanatory!)

Socorro is used for *help/aid/assistance/relief*:
¡Socorro!   Help! (when called out loud)
Trabajos de Socorro.   Relief/rescue work.
Linked words:
Socorrer.   To help (person), to meet (need), to relieve, to bring aid to.
Socorrido/a.   Well-stocked/handy/helpful/obliging.
El socorrismo.   Life-saving.
Un/a socorrista.   Lifeguard/life-saver.

Auxilio is used for *help/aid/assistance* which generally is associated with a medical context but that does not necessarily have to be the case:

Primeros auxilios.   First aid.

Acudir en auxilio de alguien.   To come to somebody's *aid*.

El auxilio social.   Social welfare.

Linked words:

Auxiliar (adj).   Assistant/auxiliary/ancillary.

El/la auxiliar (noun).   Assistant.

Auxiliar de vuelo.   Air steward/stewardess.

Auxiliar (verb).   To help/assist/to attend (a dying person)/to aid/give aid to (politically).

Other words which can be used in the context of helping:

Una asistenta.   Daily help.

El médico me dió algo para aliviar el dolor.   The doctor gave me something to *help/relieve* the pain.

No hay más remedio.   It is beyond *help*/there's nothing to be done/It can't be *helped*.

De nada sirve ponerte así.   *It is no help* being like that.

Servirse.   To *help* oneself (to food).

No lo puedo evitar/¿Qué quieres que haga?   I *can't help* it/What do you want/expect me to do about it?

Todo ayuda.   Every little helps.

Echar una mano.   To help out.

Rapidez, velocidad, prisa – *speed*

Rapidez is a word used for *rapidity*, *speed*:

La rapidez en taquigrafía.   Shorthand *speed*.

Linked words are:

Rápidamente.   Fast, quickly.

Rápido.   Fast, quick, quickly.

Un tren rápido.   An express train.

Los rápidos.   Rapids.

Velocidad is used when the meaning of *speed* becomes *rate/pace/velocity/swiftness*:

De alta velocidad.   High-speed.

Velocidad adquirida.   Momentum.

Cobrar velocidad.   To pick up/gather speed.

Moderar la velocidad.   To slow down.
La velocidad máxima/permitida.   The speed limit.
Meter la cuarta velocidad.   To change into fourth gear.

Linked words:
Veloz.   Fast, swift.
El velocímetro.   Speedometer.

Prisa is used when the meaning of *speed* becomes *hurry/ haste/urgency*:
A/de prisa.   Quickly/hurriedly.
A toda prisa.   As quickly as possible.
Correr prisa.   To be urgent.
Esta carta corre prisa.   This is an urgent letter (needs to get to its destination urgently).
¡Date prisa!   Hurry up!/Get a move on*!*
Tener prisa.   To be in a hurry.

Also useful to know

Correr a toda prisa/apresurarse.   To speed/go fast/hurry.
Pasaron los años volando.   The years sped/flew by.
Acelerar.   To speed up/accelerate.
Una lancha motora.   Speedboat.
Un cuentakilómetros.   Speedometer.
Unas carreras de moto/una pista de carrera.   Speedway.

Hora, tiempo, vez – *time*

These nouns can all be used to mean *time*, however, once again, their meanings are all specific:

Hora is used for *time* when referring to the *time (hour) of day*:
¿Qué *hora* es?   What *time* is it (what hour of the day)?
¿A qué *hora* quedamos?   What *time* shall we meet?

Tiempo is used for *time* when the duration is somewhat vague/indefinite:
No tengo tiempo para ir de compras hoy.   *I don't have time* to go shopping today.
¡Cuánto tiempo sin verte!   Long time no see!
Cada cierto tiempo.   Every so often.

El tiempo libre.   Free/spare *time*.

Tiempo also has other meanings:

¿Cuánto tiempo tiene el pequeño ahora?   *How old* is the little one now?

El primer *tiempo* del partido.   The first *half* of the match.

Marcar el *tiempo*.   To keep the *beat* (music)/*tempo*.

El tiempo can also mean *the tense* (grammar) or refer to *the weather*!

Vez is used for *time* when referring to *occasions or different times*:

Por primera *vez*.   For the first *time*.

Esta *vez* te lo hago.   I'll do it for you this *time*/just this once.

Érase una *vez*.   Once upon a *time*.

Vez can also be used for *turn/place*.

A su *vez*.   In her *turn*.

Ceder la *vez*.   To give up one's *turn/place*.

Note also:

A la vez.   At one and the same time.

En vez de.   Instead of.

Trabajo, tarea, obra – *work*

Trabajo is the most commonly used word for *work*, coming from the verb *trabajar* (to work). It can also mean a *job/task*.

Tiene un *trabajo* fijo.   She has a permanent *job*.

Trabajo por/de/en turno.   Shift work.

Los sin trabajo.   The unemployed.

Estar sin trabajo.   To be unemployed.

Trabajo eventual.   Casual work.

Linked words:

Trabajado/a.   Carefully worked or worn out.

Trabajador/a.   Hard-working.

Trabajosamente.   Laboriously/painfully.

Trabajoso/a.   Hard/laborious/painful.

Tarea is used when the work referred to is more of a *job/task/chore*:

Tengo que hacer las *tareas de la casa.*   I have to do the *housework/household chores.*

Es una *tarea* poco grata.   It's a thankless *task.*

Obra is used more when the idea is of a *piece of work*:

Una obra de arte.   A *work* of art.

¡Manos a la obra!   Let's get to *work*/get to it/get started!

Las *obras* completas de Antonio Machado.   The complete *works* of Antonio Machado.

Una obra de teatro.   A (theatrical) play/work.

"Obras".   Building under construction/men at work (on roads).

Cerrado por obras.   Closed for repairs/alterations.

Linked words:

El obrador.   Workshop (L. Am.).

El obraje.   Sawmill/timberyard (L. Am.) and, in Mexico, a pork butcher's (shop).

El obrajero.   Lumberman/craftsman/skilled worker (L. Am.) and, as above, a pork butcher.

Obrar.   To work/have an effect on (medically)/to act/behave.

Obrar de acuerdo con.   To act in accordance with.

In Latin America *obrar* can also mean 'to have a bowel movement'!

Also useful to know

Other words which can be used to translate an idea of *work*: *esfuerzo*

Le ha puesto grandes *esfuerzos.*   She has put a lot of *work/effort* into it.

Faena for the idea of 'task':

Estar en plena faena.   To be hard at work.

Faenar.   To work/labour.

Empleo for the idea of 'employment/job':

Estar desempleado/parado/en paro.   To be unemployed.

Estoy de baja esta semana.   I am off work (ill) this week.

The verb *trabajar* (to work) also has its own set of alternatives: *funcionar/marchar/andar.*   To work/function/go.

Note also:

Trabajo de chinos.   Hard slog.

Trabajo a destajo.   Piecework.

Trabajos forzados.   Hard labour.

Trabajos manuales.   Handicrafts.

Ahorrarse el trabajo.   To save oneself the trouble.

Me cuesta trabajo hacerlo.   I find it very hard to do.

Dar trabajo.   To cause trouble.

Hacer una faena a alguien.   To play a dirty trick on someone.

Una faena (in bull-fighting).   A series of passes with the cape.

Un faenaro (Chile).   Farm worker.

Poner algo por obra.   To carry something out.

Obras son amores y no buenas razones.   Actions speak louder than words.

Seguro que es obra tuya.   I am sure this is your doing.

Connectors

Y vs E – *and*

Both these conjunctions mean *and* with **y** being much more familiar to all and sundry. The basic rule is: always use **y** unless the word following it begins with *i* or *hi*, which is when **e** should be used.

Mi niña es bonita *e* inteligente.   My little girl is both pretty *and* intelligent.

Padre *e* hijo/madre *e* hija.   Father *and* son/mother *and* daughter.

¿Cómo se llaman los gemelos? Francisca *e* Isabel.   What are the twins called? Francisca *and* Isabel.

Pero vs sino – *but*

Pero is the word most used to translate *but*. However, when the sentence which precedes the word *but* is a negative one, *but* should be translated by **sino** (*but rather*).

Me gusta la falda *pero* no me gusta el color.   I like the skirt *but* I don't like the colour.

No me gusta la falda *sino* la camiseta.   I don't like the skirt *but* (rather) the t-shirt.

Para, por – *for*

Again, there is a common difficulty to overcome here in a non-native speaker's quest for fluency.

First, let's get rid of any possible confusion:

– they do not both only mean *for*

– *por* looks and sounds like *for* but is not its only meaning

– if you have previously learnt French, *por* can be confused with *pour* (which does mean *for*), but a more general rule is that *por* is closer to the French *par* and *para* is closer to the French *pour*.[2]

Both words can mean *for* but **para** is the one more often used to mean *intended for, destined for, in order to, towards* and for expressions of time,

Este regalo es *para* tí.   This gift is (intended) *for* you.

Es el tren *para* Segovia.   It is the Segovia train (*destination*).

Lo hago ahora *para* no tener que hacerlo más tarde.   I am doing it now *so as* not to have to do it later.

Lo he pedido *para* mañana.   I have ordered it *for* tomorrow.

Seguimos el camino *para* el norte.   Let's head (*for the*) north.

Hablar *para* sí.   To talk *to* oneself (intended for your ears only!)

¿*Para* qué sirve esto?   What *use* is this/does this have?

Por, on the other hand, only occasionally means *for* and has several other meanings: *so as to, because of, judging by, in/by, according to, by wayof/through, in exchange for, on behalf of* and *as/per*. It is also used in many set phrases, to express time in the present and future, and for approximate dates:

Por no quedar fuera del juego, el niño se dedicó a seguir las reglas.   *So as* not to be out of the game, the boy followed the rules.

Por causa de la lluvia hoy, vamos mañana.   *Because of* the rain today, let's go tomorrow.

---

[2] Phil Turk and Mike Zollo, (Ibid)

Me gustaría viajar *por* toda España.   I would love to travel *throughout* Spain.

Con mi madre le hablo *por* teléfono todos los días.   I speak to my mother *on* the phone every day.

Vamos, niños, hay un helado *por* persona.   Come along, children, there is one ice-cream *per* person.

Estaremos de vacaciones *por* un mes.   We will be on holiday *for* a month.

Por la mañana/tarde/noche.   *In* the morning/afternoon/evening.

Por si acaso.   Just in case.

Por todas partes.   Everywhere.

Por Navidad/Semana Santa.   *At* Christmas/Easter.

Por ejemplo.   *For* example.

Por supuesto.   Of course.

Por fin/por último.   At last, finally.

Por ahora.   *For* now.

Por cierto.   Certainly.

Por completo.   Completely.

Por lo común.   Usually.

Por consecuencia/consiguiente.   Consequently.

Por culpa de.   The fault of.

Por lo demás.   Furthermore.

Por dentro y por fuera.   Inside and out.

Por desgracia.   Unfortunately.

Por escrito.   In writing.

Por eso/por lo tanto.   Therefore, that's why.

Por favor.   Please.

Por lo general.   Generally.

Por lo menos.   At least.

Por primera vez.   For the first time.

Por lo mismo.   For that very reason.

Por lo que a mí/por mi parte.   As far as I am concerned.

Por lo visto.   Apparently.

Por poco.   Almost.

Por su cuenta.   Alone/on one's own.

Por un lado . . . por otro.   On the one hand . . . on the other.

Some verbs also carry the preposition *por* as part of their make-up:

Acabar por.   To end up doing.
Empezar por.   To begin by doing.
Interesarse por.   To be interested in.
Luchar por.   To fight/strive for/to.
Preguntar por alguien.   To ask for/about/after someone.
Preocuparse por/de algo/alguien.   To worry about something/someone.
Quedar por.   To remain to be done.
Terminar por.   To end by doing.

O vs U – *or*

Both these conjunctions mean *or* and **o** is the one that most of us are much more at ease using. The basic rule is: always use **o** unless the word coming directly after it begins with *o* or *ho*, which is when **u** should be used. (Admittedly, if you pause long enough when speaking, between the two *o* sounds, you could get away without anyone noticing that you hadn't switched letters . . . but let's not get into bad habits!)

¿Es para chicos *u* hombres?   Is it for boys *or* men?
No me acuerdo si fue en septiembre *u* octubre cuando se marchó.   I can't remember if it was in September *or* October when he left.

When written, **o** has an accent if it is between two numerals so as to distinguish it clearly from the numbers themselves:
¿Me dijo 20 *ó* 21€?   Did you say 20 *or* 21 euros?

Entonces, luego, así que, pues, es decir, de modo que, de manera que, con/por lo cual – *so*

When *so* is used to link one phrase to another, it has many levels of formality and subtleties of meaning:

Entonces/luego can both mean then. *Entonces* can also mean at that time, at that point, in that case or in such circumstances.
Pues entonces ('Well, then') is used at the start of a sentence to refer to what has already been said.

Luego is a little more restricted to time so *Pues luego* ('Well, after that') at the start of a sentence refers to what is about to be said.

Primero voy a hacer las compras y *luego* iremos al parque ¿vale?   First I am going to do the shopping and *then* we'll go to the park, OK?

Luego can also mean *later/in a minute/afterwards*:

Hasta luego.   See you later (see notes on 'goodbye' on page 82/3).

Luego.   Therefore/so.

Desde luego (mainly in Spain).   Of course /certainly/ naturally. (In Latin America this would be *por supuesto*).

Así que. *So/therefore* (a kind of summing up).

Así que has dejado de fumar.   *So* you've given up smoking.

Así que no queda pastel para mí ¡qué bien!   *So* there's no cake left for me, great!

Pues – then, well (then), so

Pues si la situación es así no voy.   *Well*, if the situation's like that, I'm not going.

¿Pues?   So? Well?

Pues can also be used to indicate some form of consequence (*since*):

Anda, cómpralo *pues* lo quieres tanto.   Go on, buy it *as/ since* you want it so much.

Es decir – that is to say, I mean

Es decir is really a much more formal way of saying *so*.

No me gusta esa chica, *es decir*, me da algo sólo con verla.   I don't like that girl, *I mean*, I just can't stand to look at her.

Las cosas van de mal en peor, *es decir* de verdad tenemos que hacer algo.   Things are going from bad to worse, *that is to say*, we must act now.

De modo que. *So* (but even more formal!)

¡De modo que fuiste tú de veras!   *So* it really was you!

De manera que. *So* (that)

De manera que ¿no te gusta, entonces?   *So* you don't like it, then?

Pinté la casa *de manera que* le gustara a todos.   I painted the house to everyone's liking/*so that* everyone liked it.

Con/por lo cual. *At which, whereupon, because (of the fact that), so, on account of*

Llegué tarde a la fiesta *con lo cual* no me dejaron entrar.   I arrived late for the party *so* they would not let me in.

Los fuegos artificiales fueron muy ruidosos *por lo cual* era mejor guardar los animales en casa.   The fireworks were very loud *so* it was best to keep the animals indoors.

Helping you learn

Progress checks

1 Looking at the English side only, translate a whole section into Spanish and check your answers.
2 Read a passage in Spanish (in a textbook, magazine or newspaper) and see if you can spot any of the problem words or phrases.
3 Write down Spanish words to translate the English ones mentioned and check your answers.

Discussion points

1 Find out if your fellow students have difficulties with the same words and phrases found in this chapter and explain them to each other.
2 Never miss the opportunity to get a native speaker to explain to you the differences between similar words and phrases.
3 Do you agree that the complexity of any language is what makes it more interesting to learn?

Practical assignment

Test your fellow students and let them test you on the difficulties covered in this chapter.

Study tips
Never expect to say everything perfectly the first time around in Spanish; be prepared to experiment!

3 Choosing the right word - 2

One-minute overview

In this chapter the aim is to consider *false cognates*, often known as *false friends* or *unreliable friends* (words which may sometimes mean the same in English and sometimes not). As English contains such a large amount of Latin, many Spanish words are assumed to have a particular meaning because they look like a similar word in English. *Ilusión, decepción, comprometer, pretender, desgracia* and *contestar* are just some of the ones that spring to mind. The total list of these words is enormous so the lists have been separated out to include a few of the ones you will meet regularly and others which are perhaps a little less common.

Everyday false friends (*falsos amigos*)

These include: *acostar, actual, anciano, antiguo, arena, asistir, atender, auditorio, bizcocho, campo, carbón, carpeta, carta, chocar, collar, cómodo, conferencia, confianza, confidencia, constipado, consulta, contestar, convenir, decepción, desmayo, devolver, diario, divisar, editor, efectivamente, embarazada, emocionante, esperar, espina, eventual, éxito, fábrica, genial, idioma, jubilarse, largo, lectura, librería, maleta, mantel, mayor, noticia, pariente, particular, pasar, pastel, profesor, realizar, recordar, regalar, sano, sensible, simpático, soportar, suspender, tinta, tormenta, trampa, vaso.*

Acostar(se) does not mean 'to accost' but rather *to put to bed/go to bed*. Note the difference between *estar acostado* and *estar en cama*: the former implies that someone has gone to bed of their own accord while the latter suggests an underlying problem (illness, unusual time of day). 'To accost' is translated most closely by *abordar*.

Actual does not mean 'actual' but rather *present/current*. 'Actually' can be translated by *realmente/en realidad*. 'In actual fact' would then be *en la realidad/concretamente*.

Anciano does not mean 'ancient' but rather *old/aged* and when it is used with the article, *el/la anciano/a,* it means the *old man/woman*. 'Ancient' would be translated by *antiguo/a/viejísimo/a* or even plain old *histórico/a*.

Antiguo/a does not mean 'antique' but rather *ancient/old/former/senior*. 'Antique' would be better translated by *clásico/a/de época* and even better still by *antigüedad* when used as a noun.

Arena does not mean an 'arena' but rather refers to *sand*. 'Arena' would be better translated by *estadio* (stadium)/*plaza* (bullfighting)/*ruedo* (political)/*pista* (circus)/*palestra* (stage).

Asistir does not mean 'to assist' but rather *to attend/be present at*. Note also: *la asistencia* usually means 'audience/those attending', *un asistente* usually means 'attendant/anyone present', but in the army it can mean an 'orderly' and *una asistenta* can mean a 'daily help/home help'. 'To assist' is better translated by *ayudar*.

Atender does not mean 'to attend/be present' but rather *to attend to/take care of*.

Auditorio does not just mean an *auditorium/hall*; it can also mean an *audience*.

Bizcocho does not mean 'biscuit' but rather *sponge cake* or *bun*. 'Biscuit' would be translated as *galleta*.

Campo does not just mean *camp* but also refers to *a field* or *the countryside*. 'Camp' would usually be translated by *un camping/campamento*.

Carbón does not just mean *carbon* but also refers to *coal* or *charcoal*. Another word for 'carbon' is *carbono*.

Carpeta does not mean 'carpet' but has several meanings throughout the Spanish-speaking world. In Spain and Mexico it means *file* or *briefcase*. In Peru it means a *school* *desk* (elsewhere known as *un pupitre*). In Colombia it can refer to a sort of *table cloth*. 'Carpet' is *alfombra* and, if wall-to-wall, *moqueta*.

Carta does not mean a 'card' but rather a *letter*. 'Card/postcard' would be translated as *tarjeta*. The material 'card' would be translated as *cartón*. *La cartilla* is increasingly being used to refer to some form of *identity card*.

Chocar does not mean 'to shock' but rather *to collide with/bump into* a solid object. If a person is involved, however, the translation is usually *atropellar*. The verb 'to shock' is translated by *escandalizar/dar un susto*. The medical term 'to be in shock' uses the English word: *estar en shock*.

Collar does not just mean *collar* bur rather a *necklace*. 'Collar' (of a shirt) would be translated by *cuello*.

Cómodo does not mean 'commodious' or 'commodity' but rather *comfortable*. *Comodidades* means 'creature comforts' and the Spanish for 'commodities' is *géneros/mercancías*. However a hotel with *muchas comodidades* has many 'facilities'.

Conferencia does not mean 'conference' but rather a *lecture* or, in Spain, a *long-distance telephone call*. In Latin America it can be used to mean *an interview*. 'A conference' is translated by *un congreso*.

Confianza does not just mean 'confidence' but also 'trust', 'reliance' and even 'familiarity'. Note: *de confianza* means 'trustworthy/honest' so *un amigo de confianza* is 'a close friend'.

Confidencia does not, therefore just mean *confidence* but also *secret/trust*.

Constipado does not mean 'constipated' but rather *to have a cold/be blocked up/have a blocked nose*. In Latin America *resfriado* is more often used. 'Constipated' is translated by *estreñido*.

Consulta does not just mean *consultation* but can also mean *enquiry* and, in medical terms, a *surgery/consulting room* or even an *examination*.

Contestar does not mean 'to contest' but rather *to answer/ reply*. In Latin America *responder* is more common. 'To contest' is translated by *disputar/impugnar*.

Convenir does not mean 'to convene' but rather *to agree/ fit/suit/be suitable*. 'To convene' is translated by *convocar/ reunirse*.

Decepción does not mean 'deception' but rather *disappointment*. 'Deception' is translated by *engaño*.

Desmayo does not mean 'dismay' but rather a *faint/swoon*. 'Dismay' is not easily translated and often the idea of *mala sorpresa or desengaño* is used.

Devolver does not mean 'to devolve', or have any connection with 'devolution', but rather *to pay/give back*. 'To devolve on' is most closely translated by *recaer en/pasar a/incumbir a*.

Diario does not just mean *daily* but, as in English, has adopted the meaning of a *daily newspaper/journal* and even a *diary*. Another way to translate *daily* as meaning 'day-to-day' would be *cotidiano/a* or *de cada día*.

Divisar does not mean 'to devise' but rather *to make out/perceive/distinguish*. 'To devise' is translated by *concebir/ inventar/elaborar/tramar*.

Editor does not just mean *editor* but also *compiler/ publisher*. Note, by the same token, *editorial* does not always mean 'editorial' but is often short for *una casa editorial* meaning 'a publishing house'. An editor of a newspaper is translated by *el/la redactor/a* and, in the context of radio, TV or cinema, *un/a montador/a*.

Efectivamente does not mean 'effectively' but rather *in effect* and can also be used for a resounding *yes* or even the word *actually*. 'Effective' is translated by *eficaz* and 'effectively' by *eficazmente*.

Embarazada does not mean 'embarrassed' but rather *pregnant* and is therefore not often found in a masculine form of the adjective! 'Embarrassed' or 'uncomfortable' is translated by *avergonzado/a*, *apenado/a* or *puesto/a en un aprieto*.

Emocionante does have a link with 'emotion' (*emoción*) but, as we do have a tendency to exaggerate as human beings, such words are often used when we actually mean 'excitement/to get excited'. Thus *emocionante* is more commonly used to mean *exciting/thrilling* and, equally, *emocionado* to mean *excited/worked up*. However, a word of warning: these words, in certain contexts, can also have sexual connotations and the word 'excited' is generally a very difficult word to translate into Spanish, given that emotions are very subjective terrain. If the meaning is 'moved', then a better word would be *conmovido/a* but check also *excitar* (to get highly excited or even stimulated), *inquieto/a* (fidgety/jumpy) or *nervioso/a* (highly-strung/nervy/excitable).

Esperar is not automatically the verb used for 'to expect' but, more commonly, the verb *to hope/wait for*. 'To expect' can be translated by *suponer/imaginar* or *estar embarazada/encinta* (to be expecting a baby).

Espina does not automatically mean *spine* but also *thorn/splinter* or *bone of a fish*. 'Spine' as in 'backbone' can also be *espinazo* or *columna vertebral*. Linked words are:
La espinilla.   Shinbone, (Med.) blackhead.
La espinillera.   Shinpad/guard.
El espino.   Hawthorn.
Espinoso/a.   Thorny/prickly/bony/knotty.
El espinoso.   Stickleback.
Note:
Me da mala espina.   It makes me suspicious.
Sacarse la espina.   To get even.
Doblar el espinazo.   To knuckle under.

Eventual(mente) does not mean 'eventually' as in 'ultimately' but rather *possibly* and always depending upon chance events. 'Eventually' would be translated as *por último/finalmente*.

Éxito does not mean 'exit' but rather *success*. 'Exit' is translated by *salida*.

Fábrica does not mean 'fabric' but rather *factory*. 'Fabric' as in a form of textile is translated by *tejido/tela* and the 'fabric' of a building would be *la estructura*.

Genial does not mean 'genial' but rather, as an adjective, 'brilliant/of genius' and as an exclamation 'fantastic/marvellous/wonderful'. 'Genial' is translated in a number of ways: *cordial*, *sociable*, *cariñoso*, *afable* depending on the context.

Idioma (*masc.*) does not mean 'idiom', as in a particular expression familiar to a particular language, but rather the *language* spoken by a particular nation. The words *lenguaje* and *lengua* are also used but their meanings are slightly more specific in that *lenguaje* refers to particular uses of a given language and *lengua* refers to *tongue* both literally and in reference to a vernacular spoken within a main language. The word for 'idiom' is *un modismo/una locución*.

Jubilarse/jubilación does not refer to any form of 'jubilation' but rather to *to retire/retirement*. 'Jubilation' can be translated by *júbilo* (not very common), *alegría* or *regocijo*.

Largo does not mean 'large' (nor 'wide' as in French or Italian) but rather *long*. 'Large' would be translated by *grande* and 'wide' by *ancho*.

Lectura does not mean 'lecture' but rather *reading*. 'Lecture' is translated by *conferencia*.

Librería does not mean 'library' but rather *bookshop* or *bookcase*. A 'library' is translated by *biblioteca*.

Maleta does not mean 'mallet' but rather a *suitcase/travelling bag*. Linked words are:
Un maletero.   Boot/trunk of a car.
Un maletín.   Small case/briefcase/attaché case.
Maleta can also have other meanings, more commonly used in Latin America: *naughty/mischievous/lazy* or, as a noun, *a lazy person/saddlebag/bundle of clothes/hump*.
Thus *un maletudo.*   Hunchback.

In the world of bullfighting, *un maleta* can mean 'a clumsy beginner' and *un maletilla*, 'an aspiring bullfighter'. The word for 'mallet' is *un mazo*.

Mantel (*masc.*) does not mean 'mantle/cloak/covering' but rather a *tablecloth/covering* or, in religious terms, an *altar cloth*. The word for 'mantle' is *una capa*.

Mayor does not refer to the 'mayor' but rather is a comparative adjective used to mean *bigger/older/elder/senior/major*. The 'mayor' is *el alcalde*.

Noticia does not mean 'notice' but rather *news item*. A 'notice' is usually translated by *un aviso/anuncio*. Note 'at short notice' (*con poca antelación*), 'worthy of notice' (*digno de atención*), 'until further notice' (*hasta nuevo aviso*), '*without notice*' (*sin aviso/sin avisar*). 'To give notice' (to fire/sack) is *despedir*.

Pariente does not mean 'parent' but rather *relative/relation* (within the family). 'Parents' is translated by *padres*.

Particular does not mean 'particular' but rather *private/personal*. The best translation for 'particular' is *especial*.

Pasar can mean *to pass* but colloquially has several other meanings:
¿Qué pasa?   What's happening/going on/how are you?
¡Pase!   Come in!/After you!
Siempre pasa igual/lo mismo.   It's always the same.
Pasar tiempo.   To spend time.

Pastel (*masc.*) can be used to mean *pastel* (art) but more commonly is used to mean *cake/pastry*. Linked words:
La pastelería.   Cake shop/confectioners.
El/la pastelero/a.   Baker/confectioner.
El pastelillo.   Tart (culinary).

Profesor does not mean 'professor' but rather *teacher*. 'Professor' is translated by *catedrático* but carries less prestige in Spanish than in English. A much higher title would be that of *doctor*.

Realizar can mean *to realize* but usually in the sense of *to make something happen/achieve/fulfil/carry out*. 'To realize', in the sense of becoming aware of something, is better translated by *darse cuenta de*.

Recordar does not mean 'recorder/to record' but rather *to recall/remind*. *Recordar* and *acordarse* are almost interchangeable for *to remember* but only *recordar* will do for *to remind*. 'To record' is translated by *grabar* (onto cassette or disc), *registrar, inscibir, hacer constar* or *dejar constancia de* (in writing).

Regalar does not mean 'to regale' (oneself) but rather *to give as a gift*. *Un regalo* means *a present*. 'To regale (oneself)' is translated by *darse el lujo de*.

Sano does not mean 'sane' but rather *healthy/sound/whole(some)*. The phrase *sano y salvo* means *safe and sound*. 'Sane' is translated by *cuerdo/a or sabio/a*.

Sensible does not mean 'sensible' but rather *sensitive* (of people) and *considerable/appreciable* (of things). 'Sensible' is translated by *sensato/práctico*. *La sensible* is the seventh note of the scale in musical terms.

Simpático does not mean 'sympathetic' but rather *nice/easy to get on with/of a friendly disposition*. 'To sympathise' would be best translated by *compadecer*.

Soportar does not always mean 'to support' unless used figuratively to mean *to put up with/endure/stand/bear* (note also the possibility of using *aguantar*).
'To support' can be translated by *apoyar/sostener* (physically/emotionally)/*aprobar* (in favour of)/*seguir* (football team)/*confirmar* (evidence)/*respaldar*.
Note: *ganarse la vida* means 'to support oneself' (financially).

Suspender can mean *to suspend/hang up* and also means *to fail* (test/exams).

Tinto/tinta does not mean 'tint' but rather, adjectivally, *stained/dyed* or *red* (of wine) or even *black* (of coffee in Colombia).

Linked words:

La tinta. Ink.

Tintar. To dye.

El tinte. Dye/tinge/colouring/dry cleaners.

El tintero. Inkwell/pot.

La tintorería. Dry cleaners.

El tintorro. Cheap red wine/plonk.

'Tint' is better translated by *tono/matiz* and as *teñir* for 'to tint'.

Tormenta does not mean 'torment' but rather *storm/ thunderstorm*. 'Torment' would be translated by *tormento (masc.)/suplicio*.

Trampa does not mean a 'female tramp'! It is better translated as a more colloquial word for *trick/racket/fiddle/con*.

Hacer trampas. To cheat.

'A tramp' is best translated by the words *vagabundo/a* or *vago/ a* and, in a pejorative sense, *una zorra* (she sleeps around).

Vaso does not mean 'vase' but rather *glass/tumbler*. 'A vase' would be translated by *un florero/un jarrón*. However, *un vaso* in Peru can also mean *a hub cap* and note that *un vaso de noche* can mean *a chamber pot* although *un orinal* is more commonly the translation. Remember also that a 'glass of wine' is *una copa de vino* (usually a glass with a stem).

Less common false friends

These include: *advertir, agonía, apología, bachiller, bagaje, bala, barraca, bizarro, calificar, cargo, chanza, colorado, complexión, condescender, delito, desgracia, destituir, destreza, disgusto, distinto, divulgación, equivocar, extenuar, injuria, intoxicado, labrador, lujuria, mesura, oración, ordinario, palo, pinchar, pretender, prospecto, pupilo, rato, refrán, remover, restar, sancionar, suburbio, suceder, tabla, voluble*.

Advertir does not mean 'advert' nor 'to avert' nor 'to advertise' nor 'to advise' but rather *to give notice of/warning of/to inform*. It is commonly used in business letters: les *advertimos* que . . . (we would *advise/inform* you that . . .) and may contain an element of warning (although not always a very serious one). Note: *te advierto que* ('mind

you/do you realize that') and when a serious warning is required *dar advertencia* is much more appropriate: *Le doy advertencia.*   Mark my words.
'Advert' is translated by *un anuncio*; 'to avert' by *apartar/prevenir/bloquear*, 'to advertise' by *anunciar/hacer publicidad* and 'to advise' by *aconsejar*.

Agonía does not mean 'agony/great pain' but rather *dying breath*. Note *en su agonía* (on his death bed). There is no one word in Spanish for 'agony' so phrases such as *un dolor horrible/terrible/agudo* would have to suffice.

Apología does not mean 'apology' unless it is in the legal meaning of *apologia* in English, which means a 'formal written defence' of a cause. It is not a very common word in Spanish and *defensa* or *justificación* are more likely to be used in its place.
The translation for 'apology' is more likely to be *disculpa/excusa* (see p. 83-85).

Bachiller/a does not mean 'bachelor' but rather a *secondary-school graduate*. Linked with this is the word *el bachillerato* which is the equivalent of the *British GCSE system* (exams at age 16).
The word for *bachelor* would be *soltero/a* (unmarried) or *licenciado/a* (with a Bachelor's degree).

Bagaje can be used to mean *baggage/equipment* but it can also mean *experience* or *background*. A more common translation for 'baggage' would be *equipaje*.

Bala does not mean 'ball' but rather *bullet*. A 'ball' is translated by *pelota/bola/balón* (sport)/*ovillo* (wool)/*pulpejo* (of the foot)/*baile* (dance).

Barraca does not mean 'barracks' but rather *hut/cabin*. 'Barracks' is translated by *cuartel* (Spain) or *caserna* (L. Am.). Note that a ship's cabin is *un camarote*.

Bizarro/a does not mean 'bizarre' but rather *gallant/brave/generous*. 'Bizarre' would best be translated by *raro/a* or *extraño/a* or *estrafalario/a* (eccentric).

Calificar does not mean 'to qualify' but rather *to mark/grade* or *to describe (as)*. 'To qualify (for a post)' would be translated by *tener los requisitos/títulos para un puesto* and 'to qualify (modify/tone down)' by *modificar*, *suavizar* or *atenuar*.

Cargo does not mean 'cargo' but rather *load/weight/burden*; *charge/debit* (commercially); *post/office* (job); *duty/ responsibility* (obligation); and *charge/care* (safekeeping). Linked words:
Cargar.   To load with/burden/weigh down/impose.
A cargo de.   In the charge of.
Jurar el cargo.   To take the oath of office/be sworn into office.
'Cargo' is best translated into Spanish by *cargamento/carga*.

Chanza does not mean 'chance' but rather *joke*.
Chanzas.   Fun.
De/en chanza.   In fun/as a joke.
Estar de chanza.   To be joking.
'Chance' is best translated by *suerte/azar* (luck); *casualidad* (coincidence); *oportunidad* (chance/opportunity); or *posibilidad/riesgo*.

Colorado/a can literally mean *coloured* but unless the colour in question is specified, it means *red*.
Ponerse colorado/a.   To blush.
'Coloured' can be translated by *de color/de muchos colores/ de grancolorido* and, if referring to someone's skin colour, *de color/negro/a*.

Complexión does not mean 'complexion' but rather 'build' (of a person). As 'complexion' in English most often applies to the face, this would be translated by *el cutis/la tez*. Note also the figurative use as in 'That puts a different complexion on the matter', which can be translated as *Eso le da otro aspecto*.

Condescender does not mean 'to condescend' but rather 'to acquiesce/be obliging/submit'. *Condescendente* therefore means to be 'obliging/submissive/complaisant'. 'To condescend' is translated by *dignarse* but note that there is no corresponding adjective.

Delito does not mean 'delight' but rather a *crime/offence/misdeed*. 'Delight' is best translated by *alegría/deleite/goce/regocijo/encanto*.
Para mi gusto y placer.   To my delight.

Desgracia does not mean 'disgrace' but rather *misfortune*.
¡Qué desgracia!   How unfortunate!/What bad luck!
'Disgrace' is translated by *vergüenza*.

Destituir does not mean 'destitute' but rather *to dismiss from office* (in politics). 'Destitute' is translated by *indigente*.

Destreza does not mean 'distress' but rather *dexterity/skill/nimbleness/agility* (from Latin *dexteritas*). 'Distress' has several possible meanings in English and therefore several possible translations: *angustia* (anguish)/*miseria* (poverty)/*apuro* (embarrassment).

Disgusto does not mean 'disgust' but rather *displeasure* and usually is in a verbal phrase and carrying the indefinite article: *llevarse un disgusto* (to be upset). 'Disgust' is not an easy word to translate into Spanish because, once again, it often depends on the context of the situation. Words such as *vergüenza* (morally disgusted) or *asco/desprecio/repulsión* spring to mind.

Distinto does not mean 'distinct' but rather *different* although *diferente* is also used. 'Distinct' is translated by *visible/claro/destacado*.

Divulgación does not have anything to do with divulging secrets but rather means *dissemination/broadcasting/making facts widely known*. 'To divulge' would best be translated by *revelar*.

Equivocar(se) does not mean 'to equivocate' but rather *to mistake/make a mistake*. 'To equivocate' is used infrequently in English, and often incorrectly, so translations of it are often very poor: *ser evasivo/vacilar* (L. Am.) are possibly the closest.

Extenuar does not mean 'to extenuate' but rather *to weaken/emaciate/exhaust*. 'To extenuate' is translated by *atenuar*. Note *circunstancias atenuantes* (extenuating circumstances).

Injuria does not mean 'injury' but rather *insult/cursing/ bad-mouthing* and is usually used in the plural. An 'injury' is translated into Spanish by *una herida* (external) or *una lesión* (internal). Non-physical damage is translated by *daño* or *perjuicio*.

Intoxicado does not mean 'intoxicated with drink', as in English, but rather *poisoned by food* (coming from its roots in *toxic*). 'Intoxicated' (with drink) is translated by *ebrio/ borracho*.

Labrador does not just mean our furry friend the Labrador dog but also a *farmer*! Linked words:
Labradío/labrantío. Arable.
El labrado. Cultivated land.
La labranza. Cultivation/work.
Labrar. To work/farm/till (land).
Un/a labriego/a. Farmhand.

Lujuria does not mean 'luxury' but rather one of the seven deadly sins: *lust.* 'Luxury' is translated by *lujo* so always make sure you stay in *un hotel de lujo!*

Mesura does not mean 'measure' but rather *calm/ moderation/restraint/courtesy.*
Linked words:
Mesurado/a. Calm/restrained/courteous.
Mesurar. To restrain/temper/measure.
'Measure' is best translated by *medida* or the verb *medir*.

Oración does not mean 'oration' but rather *prayer* and, in a grammatical context, *a sentence*. Note *partes de la oración* (parts of speech). The best way to translate 'oration' is by *discurso*.

Ordinario does not mean 'ordinary' but rather *rude/ common* (of a person). 'Ordinary' is best translated by *normal/corriente/regular*.

Palo does not mean 'pale' and is not even an adjective, but rather is a noun meaning *stick/post/pole/club (golf)*.
De tal palo tal astilla. A chip off the old block.

Estar hecho un palo. To be thin as a rake.
Pala, on the other hand, means a *spade/shovel*.
Una pala matamoscas. Fly swat.
The word 'pale' is best translated by *pálido/a* or *claro/a*.

Pinchar does not mean 'to pinch' but rather *to prick/pierce/ puncture/prod.* Figuratively speaking, it can mean *to get at/annoy* or even *to fail/suffer a defeat/get beaten.* Linked words:
Un pinchazo. Prick/jab/pang *and* a puncture/flat tyre.
Pincharse. To inject oneself.
Un pincho. Point/prickle/thorn/spike.
To pinch is translated by *pellizcar* (with fingers)/*apretar* (of shoes).

Pretender does not mean 'to pretend' but rather *to aim to/hope to/try to.* 'To pretend' has more than one possible translation: *fingir/aparentar/hacer como si —/ hacerse el —.*

Prospecto does not mean 'prospect' but rather *prospectus.* 'Prospect', again dependent upon its context, has several possible translations: *vista/panorama* (of scenery); 'What a prospect!' *!Qué futuro!* or *!Qué esperanza!* in Argentina and Uruguay.

Pupilo does not mean 'pupil' but rather a *ward* or *minor* (often an orphan) looked after, for administrative purposes, by an older person. The word for 'pupil' (school child) is translated by *alumno/a* and for 'pupil' (eye) by *la pupila.* Note the latter is also the feminine form of *pupilo.*

Rato does not mean 'rat' but rather a *period of time/while.* 'Rat' is translated by *una rata.*

Refrán does not mean 'refrain' (musical chorus) but rather *a saying/proverb.* The chorus of a song (refrain) is translated by *estribillo.*

Remover does not mean 'to remove' but rather *to stir* (culinary)/*to turn over/dig over* (garden). 'To remove' is best translated by *quitar.*

Restar does not mean 'to rest' but rather *to subtract/deduct* (maths) or *to return service* (tennis). 'To rest' is translated by *descansar*.

Sancionar does not mean 'to sanction' (permit) but rather the opposite, *to prosecute*. 'To sanction' is best translated by *autorizar*.

Suburbio does not mean 'suburb' (with English connotations of wealth) but rather *outskirts/suburb* with Hispanic connotations of poverty. The phrase *high-class suburbs* (a direct contradiction in the Hispanic world) is best translated by *colonia/urbanización*. A good translation with no connotation is *afueras* (simply the outlying areas of a town or city).

Suceder does not mean 'to succeed' but rather *to happen*. Note that a 'success' is translated by *éxito*, which is another false friend.

Tabla does not mean 'table' (perhaps, at most, a trestle table) but rather *board/plank/slab*. A *tablet of stone* might be referred to as *una tabla* but only if lying horizontally; placed vertically (and probably fixed to a wall), it would be called *una placa*. 'Table' is translated by *mesa*.

Voluble does not mean 'voluble' (fluent) but rather *easily moved about* (prices)/*changeable* (people). 'Voluble' can be translated by *locuaz/hablador/facundo*. Note *la facundia*   the gift of the gab!

Helping you learn

Progress checks

1 Write down the English translations of some of these problem words and check your answers.
2 When listening to/reading authentic Spanish, concentrate on how these problem words are used.
3 Listen to the different ways of saying things and check how these problem words are used.

Discussion points

1 Find out if fellow students are having the same difficulties with these words.
2 How important is understanding subtle differences in a language in order to avoid upsetting those you are talking to?
3 Discuss with a native speaker the difficulties of learning when you have to take false friends into account.
4 Do you agree that English has a lot of its own difficulties?

Practical assignments

1 Discuss with fellow students possible problems with using the *falsos amigos* explained in this chapter.
2 Try to spot when these words are used exactly.
3 Ask fellow students to test you.

Study tips
1 Use all the Spanish you know at every opportunity.
2 If given the chance to stay with/speak to a Spanish family, say yes!
3 Read something in Spanish every day.
4 Never give up.

Practising awkward words and phrases - 1

The richness of Spanish and the full-bodied expressions used by its people are often something that non-native speakers find hard to master. Fluency in this aspect comes from perseverance, being around Spanish speakers whenever possible and from not being afraid to make mistakes!

This chapter aims to look at the usefulness and expressiveness of the following features of the Spanish language:

- tag questions
- repetition
- exclamations
- common useful phrases.

Tag questions

When asking a question or making a statement (in either Spanish or English) to which a yes/no answer, or some form of confirmation, is required, a short phrase is added at the end of the sentence to indicate this request. This phrase is often called a 'tag' or 'tag question'.

To form the tag in English, we repeat the idea of the main statement made in a negative way (or in a positive way if the main statement is already negative):

Maria is a really nice girl, *isn't she*?

Today is Friday, *isn't it*?

You like my new dress, *don't you*?

You don't like me very much, *do you*?

To form the tag in Spanish. certain words are available to conveniently do the job for us:

María es una buena chica, *¿no?* — Maria is a nice girl, *isn't she?*

Hoy es viernes, *¿verdad?* — Today is Friday, *isn't it?*

Trabajas mucho, *¿no es verdad?* — You work a lot, *don't you?*

Repetition

As Spanish is such an expressive language, many phrases are said not once but twice (and in some cases more!). After all, why say something once if you can emphasise it and really show you mean it by saying it twice!

Two classic examples here are *sí sí* and *no no*. These can, of course, be made as emphatic as the speaker desires going from a straightforward *sí* through *sí sí, sí claro, sí por supuesto, sí claro que sí* as far as *sí claro que sí por supuesto ¿por qué no?* which, of course, to a non-Spanish speaker is far too long-winded and can only be translated by *yes, of course/yes, naturally/yes, why not?* but certainly not all three in one go!

This can also be noted with *no*, where we can have just a straightforward *no* through to *no no, no claro que no, por supuesto que no*, and so on.

Two other very common phrases which again carry an element of repetitiveness are:

de prisa y corriendo — very quickly (but, when translated, it gives the idea of not only being in a hurry to do something, but also running to do it!)

de golpe y porrazo — suddenly (but, when translated, it gives the idea of not only something having happened suddenly but having physically 'hit' you with its suddenness!)

There are several **figures of speech** and similar concepts concerning repetition in the Spanish language (apologies to all former students but the inclusion of some grammatical analysis was irresistible!).

Hypostasis – when reference is made to the essential nature of something, as opposed to its attributes, thus repeating the same idea:

Brillaba la luz.   The light shone (isn't that what lights do?).

El pez nadó en el agua.   The fish swam in the water (any other possibilities?).

Left dislocation of topic – when the speaker announces what they are going on to talk about, usually by bringing the topic forward to the beginning of the sentence or phrase to ensure that the listener knows in advance. This, again, enforces a repetition of the subject matter, which usually takes the form of a pronoun to soften the blow!

El libro que me regalaste, lo encontré muy divertido.   I found the book you bought me really fun to read. (Literally: The book you bought me, I found it fun to read). Personally I do not feel that this is good style in speech (especially in English), but there is no doubt as to its high level of effective communication.

Oxymoron – when two normally opposing concepts are joined together:

La triste alegría de la mañana.   The sad delight of the morning.

Nace una belleza terrible.   A terrible beauty is born.

Ser un mirlo blanco.   To be an impossible dream (a white blackbird).

The juxtaposition of opposites, although not true repetition, is certainly emphatic.

Pleonasm – when more words are used than is necessary to express an idea, thus quite naturally emphasising it:

Sin embargo, al mismo tiempo . . .   however, at the same time . . .

Un perrito chiquitito.   A tiny little dog.

Exclamations

Again, given the expressiveness of the Spanish language, there are lots of common exclamations which are used regularly and which can sometimes be relatively difficult to translate into English. A few of the more common ones are: *¡Anda!, ¡Vaya!, ¡Chico!, ¡Hombre!, ¡Claro!, ¡Ya!* and *¡Fíjate!*

¡Anda! / ¡Vaya!

Both these exclamations are very common.

¡Anda! usually carries a feeling of encouragement or admiration so, if someone is being persuaded to do something, *¡Anda!* takes on the meaning of 'Come on!', 'You can do it!', 'Let's hear it!' and so on. Equally, *¡Anda!* would be heard in a game of tennis, for example, meaning 'Come on!' or 'Get on with it!', if the favourite made a fault. *¡Vaya!*, on the other hand, carries a feeling of disbelief or even irritation, so in the above example of the tennis match, it might be the players themselves who exclaim *¡Vaya!* at the faults they had just served. In this instance, English translations would often be in the form of muttered self-admonition!

¡Ándale!, as with *¡Anda!*, would be used more in Latin America for positive encouragement. In Mexico and in and around Argentina and Uruguay, its use is similar to that of *chao* (see page 81) or, with a different tone of voice, 'Hurry up!', 'Get a move on!' 'Get going!', or even 'That's it!' or 'That's the one!'

¡Chico! / ¡Hombre!

¡Chico! is often used to indicate surprise and can be used in a very similar way to *¡Hombre!*

¡Hombre! and *¡Chico!* are very difficult to translate exactly into English and really reflect the characteristically animated response that a Spaniard would give to almost anything! They may be used to express emphatic or enthusiastic confirmation, mild or indignant protest, disbelief or in response to any astonishing piece of information and are often accompanied by some form of gesture (see page 113/4).

¡Hombre!¡ Ya lo creo!	I should say so! / Yes, indeed!
¡Pero, hombre!	Well I never!
¡Pero, hombre!(intonation slower)	Now see here . . .!

These exclamations are used by both sexes and all classes but they are far less used in Latin America. In the Caribbean region, *¡Manito!* is more likely to be used.

¡Claro!

A much used interjection generally meaning 'Of course' or 'Obviously'. However, according to the tone of voice employed, *¡Claro!* can imply anything from pure empathy to almost condescending irritation!

¡Y a mí me dejaron sola! *¡Claro!*   And they left me all alone! *Oh you poor thing!*

¡Y al fin, la que tenía razón fui yo! *¡Claro!*   And in the end I was right! *Of course you were!*

¿A que no quieres salir con Eduardo el feíto? *¡Claro!*   I bet you don't want to go out with ugly little Edward? *Of course not!*

¡Claro! can also be said several times during a conversation to indicate an occasional acknowledgement of what you are being told, almost the equivalent of 'Aha', 'Really?', 'You don't say' or 'Yes, I know' in English. In Chile and Peru, *¡Claro!* is almost used so much that it is becoming interchangeable with *sí*.

¡Ya!

The dictionary will give you the translations of 'already' and 'now' for *¡Ya!* but in fact it is one of the commonest words in the Spanish language and its meanings extend far beyond those just given. It is often used to show that a listener is following a conversation and agreeing. *¡Ya!* can also be used when a sudden realisation occurs and could be muttered impatiently in answer to a persistently ringing phone or doorbell:

¡Ya lo entiendo!   Now I get it!

¡Ya voy!   I'm coming!

Also useful to know

The word *ya*, when not used as an exclamation, is often used in conjunction with various verbal phrases to indicate how obvious or well known something is:

Como ya sabes.   As you know.

¡Ya lo creo!   I'll say!

¡Pues ya es algo!   Well, that's something!

It can also be used when there is a sense of being overdue
or of here and now:

Ya me voy.   Right, I'm off.

Ya es hora.   It's high time.

Ya no viene por aquí.   He doesn't come round here any
more.

¡Fíjate! / ¡Fíjase!

Again, quite a common exclamation to mean 'Just think!',
'Imagine that!' or 'Fancy that!' As before, the intonation
used to express this will give the required force of the
translated phrase.

Common useful phrases

Many of the phrases in this category begin with the ever
famous word *qué* and nearly all of them are exclamatory to
a certain degree:

¡Caramba!   Gosh!

¡Dios mío!   Good heavens!

¡Ni hablar!   No way!

¡Qué asco!   How disgusting!

¡Qué bien!   How nice!

¡Qué horror!   How awful!

¡Qué lástima!   What a pity!

¡Qué suerte!   How lucky!

¡Qué susto!   What a fright!

¡Qué pena!   What a shame!

¡Salud!   Cheers!

¡Vale!   OK!

¡De nada!   Don't mention it!

¡Menos mal!   It's just as well!

Certain words are often used to introduce an exclamation.
They will have a specific meaning in a specific context, and
be used grammatically in a particular way.

¡Cuánto! means 'how (much/many)' and is most often used
as a pronoun or an adjective:

¡Cuánto has gastado!   *What a lot* you've spent!

¡Cuánto tiempo sin verte! Well, *how long* is it since I saw you!/What a long time it's been (since I saw you)!/Long time no see!

¡Cuánto calor hace hoy! *How* hot it is today!

¡Qué . . .!
is used adjectivally to mean 'What a . . .!' or 'How . . .!' (see above examples).

¡Cómo! is used adverbially to mean 'How!' or 'What!'

¡Cómo! ¿No vas en serio? *What!* You can't be serious!

¡Cómo me lo pasé! *What* a good time I had!

¡Cómo me dió vergüenza! *How* embarrassing!/*How* embarrassed I was!

Like question words, exclamation words always carry a written accent to differentiate them from a word spelt exactly the same but serving another grammatical function. Exclamation words, when written, are always preceded by an inverted exclamation mark (see above examples), which is referred to as the *apertura* (opening) of the exclamation per se.

Helping you learn

Progress checks

1 Write down explanations given for these awkward words and phrases and check your answers.
2 Listen out for these words and phrases.
3 List the different ways of saying the same thing and check your answers.

Discussion points

1 Do you ever question oddities in your own mother tongue?
2 Why should speaking a foreign language be different?
3 Always ask a native speaker for explanations whenever the opportunity arises.

Practical assignments

1 Discuss any problematic words with fellow students.
2 Never miss the opportunity to visit a Spanish-speaking country.
3 Listen to spoken Spanish whenever possible.

Study tips
1 Speak Spanish at every opportunity.
2 Learning a foreign language is a life skill.
3 The secret of fluency is that practice makes perfect!

Practising awkward words and phrases - 2

There are some words and phrases which are particular to the Spanish language and its associated culture. These sometimes do not have direct equivalents in English and, indeed, may even be more, or less, forceful than intended when translated. As with any culture, this is often the case with swear words (see chapter 6). In Spanish, some of these words do belong to the translatable category, while others are better explained in a purely cultural context. There are yet others which, although more idiomatic, can sometimes bridge the two categories.

This chapter discusses:
- some awkward words and their translations
- awkward words with a cultural explanation
- common idioms

Some awkward words and their translations

Apodo – this word usually translates as 'nickname' but it can also be used quite legitimately for an alias or even a false name. Another word for *apodo* is *mote*.

Chisme – when used in the singular, *chisme* translates as 'thingy', 'what-d'you-call-it', etc. and in the plural as 'gossip'.

Coba – this is often translated as 'small talk' but can also mean 'flattery' and usually comes along with the verb *dar* (*dar coba a*   to flatter/suck up to).

Dios – yes, this does refer to 'God' but it is liberally used in the average Spanish conversation and, like many other phrases which have gone before, can depend entirely upon the speaker's intonation and any given situation to determine the force of its meaning. Note that *¡Por dios!* means 'For heaven's sake!' rather than 'For God's sake!'.

Fulano – this is a made-up name and is the equivalent of 'so-and-so'. Be aware, however, that when the reference is to a female, it is better to use *La señora fulana de tal* ('Mrs so-and-so') because the word *fulana* alone is a euphemism for 'whore'! Also compare 'Tom, Dick and Harry', for which the translation would be *Fulano, Zutano y Mengano*.

Funesto – because of its close links with the word 'funeral', this word is often translated as 'sad/dismal'. However, its true meaning is in fact much stronger, being that of 'disastrous/ appalling/deplorable'. Note a similarity of meaning with the word 'fatal'.

Guay – a very common exclamation to mean 'fab/brill/mega/ heavy' or whatever the current trendy word for 'fantastic' actually is!

¡Jesús! – this exclamation is often used when somebody sneezes: compare 'Bless you!'

Trámites – this is often used in a business sense to refer to all the 'red tape' and form-filling which is often involved. Can also mean 'formalities/arrangements'.

Tropecientos – this should be translated as 'umpteen' when the number of items/people being referred to is numerous but unspecified.

Awkward words with a cultural explanation

Adiós, chao, hasta . . . – goodbye

Adiós is the most well-known way of saying 'goodbye' in Spanish but note also that it can be equally used to greet someone in passing when there is no possibility of stopping to chat – almost like 'hello and goodbye' in one go!

Chao is a direct copy of the Italian word *ciao* but its popularity when saying goodbye is increasing. It is less popular in Mexico and on the Spanish mainland but not completely unknown.

Hasta . . . is probably used most widely when saying goodbye to someone but usually when a further meeting is likely:

Hasta ahora (See you very soon). Used when the next meeting is almost imminent and very often to end a telephone conversation.

Hasta pronto (See you soon). Often used in a similar situation to the above but with an element of hope being expressed.

Hasta luego (See you later). In Spain this is used especially if the next meeting is to be on the same day. In Latin America it is much more widely used to say goodbye and in fact becomes *hasta loguito* if the meeting is imminent.

Hasta mañana (See you tomorrow/in the morning). Used when the next meeting is almost definitely to be within 24 hours.

Hasta el lunes/martes . . . (See you on Monday/Tuesday . . .). Used when the next meeting is scheduled for a specific day.

Hasta la vista (See you around/when I see you). The time of the next meeting is somewhat indefinite here but the hope still remains.

These are by no means the only combinations with *hasta* and in fact it can depend entirely upon the circumstances (*hasta nunca* being a case in point where quite clearly you hope *never* to see that person again!).

Spaniards are quite thoughtful, therefore, in their leave-taking and usually communicate much more than just a simple goodbye.

Saying sorry

There are various situations which arise, both in Spanish and in English, when an *apology* is called for. This may be because you are genuinely *sorry* for having done something or said something which in some way has upset someone else; you feel *sympathy* towards someone, for example, in bereavement; you wish to *apologise for being unable to do something*, or for *admitting or disclaiming responsibility*. There are also a set of appropriate *responses to an apology*, should one be offered to you.

General apology

The verbs generally used in this context are: *pedir perdón/
disculparse*:

¡Perdón!   Sorry!

Perdóname por lo que hice.   *I'm sorry for/about* what I
did.

Perdona, se me había pasado.   *Sorry*, I clean forgot.

Perdona que no llamara antes.   *I'm sorry (that)* I didn't
ring beforehand.

Pide perdón a la Señora *por* ser tan grosero/por tu mal
comportamiento.   Ask the lady *to forgive you for* being
so rude.

Digo, *con perdón*, que es un viejo verde.   *Forgive me* for
saying so, but I think he's a dirty old man.

Perdonen las molestias.   Sorry for any inconvenience.

Disculpen si les he causado un problema.   *I apologise if*
I have caused a problem.

Expressing sympathy

Lamento mucho tus malas noticias.   *I'm very sorry* to
hear that/your bad news.

Lamento profundamente que haya pasado esto.   *I'm very
sorry* to hear what has happened.

Being unable to do something

Lo siento pero no puedo ir al cine esta noche.   *I'm sorry*
but I can't make the cinema tonight.

Siento mucho no haber podido completarlo a tiempo.   *I'm
so sorry* that I couldn't complete it on time.

Siento comunicarle que . . .   I *regret* to have to tell you
that . . .

Desgraciadamente/lamentablemente.   Unfortunately

Lo siento mucho/¡Cuánto lo siento!/Me da mucha pena
(L. Am.)   So sorry!/Awfully sorry!/Very sorry!

Admitting/disclaiming responsibility

He tenido la culpa/Es culpa mía/La culpa es mía.   It's my
fault.

Reconozco que *estaba equivocado.*   I admit that I was wrong.

Me responsabilizo plenamente de.   I *take* full *responsibility* for.

Admito que no *tenía razón.*   I admit that I *was wrong.*

No lo hice a propósito/a posta.   I didn't do it on purpose.

Ha sido *sin querer.*   It was an *accident/*I *didn't mean* to.

Dijo esas cosas *sin mala intención.*   She meant *no harm* by what she said.

Lo dije *sin darme cuenta.*   I said it *without realising/ thinking.*

No era su intención enfadarle.   He *didn't mean to* make her angry.

Espero que comprendas.   I hope you'll understand.

Replying to an apology

No pasa nada, hombre.   Don't worry about it, mate.

No te preocupes.   Don't worry (yourself) about it.

No importa.   It doesn't matter.

No tiene importancia.   It doesn't matter/It's not important.

No es ninguna molestia.   It's no trouble.

When replying after 'Thank you': *No hay problema/No hay de que.*   No problem!/No worries!/You're welcome!

Also useful to know

¡Me pagarás este comentario!   *You'll be sorry* you said that!

Compadecer/dar lástima/pena.   To feel *sorry* for.

Additional words of interest

Capicúa – the English translation for this is a *palindrome* (any wiser?). This is a word or date which is the same when said or written backwards, such as 20-11-02 or Ana.

Churro – a very general translation of this would be 'doughnut'. However, to the English speaker doughnuts are usually ring-shaped or round containing jam or cream and very sugary. A *churro* is not. Churros are certainly fried but the mixture is more like batter and any sugar is usually sprinkled on after serving; in addition, they are usually long with a slight curl as opposed to being round! They are traditionally dunked in thick hot chocolate on a Sunday after Mass and are delicious! Note that in Mexico *churro* can be a slang word for a bad film.

Criollo – historically this term was used when referring to people who were born in Latin America but of pure Spanish parentage. Over the years the term has come to refer to anything which is authentic to a specific Latin American country. It is much used in Argentina and Venezuela. The word *indígena* also exists but where *criollo* is said with pride, *indígena* can sound a little pejorative.

¡Diga! – again, particular to Spanish, this means 'Hello' but only when answering a phone call.

Gringo – not a word that is used in Spain but rather in Latin America and it probably refers to you! It usually refers to any non-local person and usually a fair-skinned one at that! As with any such term, the force with which it is said, and the context within which it is used, will belie the true force of its meaning. Anything from the now racially unacceptable terms such as 'Dago', 'Wop' and 'Kraut' through to the more tame 'Yankee', 'Brit' and 'Frenchy' or just plain old 'foreigner'!

Juerga – usually refers to some sort of boozy night out on the town! Often used with the verb *estar* (*estar de juerga*) to mean 'to be out on the town/out having fun/messing around'. Can also be used when alcohol is not involved just to mean 'playing around' and 'having fun'.

Machismo – much more common in Latin America but of equal standing in as far as being an embedded part of the Spanish-speaking cultural world. It refers to the attitude of masculinity/virility being an asset in life, or at least the importance of demonstrating such qualities openly, and is a very sexist term in today's world. Compare 'male chauvinism'.

La madrugada – a very imprecise period in the day between very late at night and very early in the morning. Compare the 'small hours'. Again, the word is dependent upon the speaker's point of view as to whether 2 am is very late at night, very early in the morning, or the night itself is still young!

La movida – another word closely linked to *juerga* but not necessarily with alcohol being involved. *La movida* usually refers, now, to the night-life of any given place and is used quite positively in most cases. Compare the phrase *¡Qué movida!* 'What a carry-on!'. The concept of *movida*, however, actually originates from the 70s drug scene and it was only later that it acquired meanings such as the cultural or social scene of certain people, or the problems of individuals or groups.

¡Olé! – this word has its roots in Arabic and is therefore deeply rooted in Spanish history. It is often said as an exclamation of appreciation during some form of performance such as a flamenco show or a bullfight. Its spontaneous timing may be compared to that of interjections of 'Praise the Lord!' or 'Alleluia' during church services or prayers.

Paella – this is one of the most typical and possibly most popular of Spanish dishes. It consists of shellfish, chicken and vegetables on a bed of rice. It is served hot and it is often a good idea to order it well in advance as any good establishment will cook the dish freshly as ordered.

Pasota – this stems from the verb *pasarse*, which means 'to be oblivious to/not to give a damn about'. *Pasota* will often refer to a person who could not care less about anything or anybody and goes through life without a care in the world! Can also be used as the equivalent of being 'laid back'.

Piropo – there is no single word in English which really translates this Hispanic phenomenon well. It refers to compliments called out (usually) to women often by admiring males and very much in public! The comments can range from anything from a simple comment on your attractiveness through to very base comments on how good your sexual performance may or may not be! The best way to react to these 'compliments' is to ignore them and keep walking because any overt encouragement may lead to an undesirable outcome! Southern Spain and Argentina are most famous for their forthrightness!

Santo – given the importance of religion in the Spanish-speaking world, most Spanish Christian names are the names of saints and every saint is allocated a day in the Christian calendar. Therefore everyone of Hispanic origin not only has a birthday to celebrate each year but also a saint's day (*santo*)! It is equally (if not more) important as the *cumpleaños* (birthday) and equally requires the giving of presents and being celebrated!

Seseo – refers to the pronunciation of the letter 'c' as if it were an 's', which is often heard in the more southern parts of the Spanish mainland and most of the Latin American countries ('55' is thus pronounced as 'sincuenta y sinco' as opposed to 'thincuenta y thinco').

Tapas – this fairly colloquial word is very often one of the first contacts that many English speakers have with the Spanish-speaking world. *Tapas* are small snacks which are often served with drinks at any respectable drinking establishment (the more refined name being *aperitivos*). However, *tapas* bars are now seen in many a British high street, where one can sample small portions of Spanish delicacies or even an à la carte menu of Spanish cuisine.

Tarde – usually translated as 'afternoon' or 'evening'. One really needs to appreciate here how the division of the day in Spanish-speaking countries is perceived. *La mañana* is usually used to refer to the period between getting up and lunchtime (although the greeting *Buenos días* almost religiously stops being used at noon) and *la tarde* then is roughly the period between noon/lunchtime and nightfall. Thus *la noche* only begins once it is dark, but note that the greeting *buenas noches* (also used for leave-taking) should only be used after nightfall. *Buenas tardes* is used for 'Good evening' while daylight prevails.

Tertulia – again, a word which has a purely cultural context and not one with any really satisfactory translation in most dictionaries. It refers to a social gathering or meeting of friends usually with a central speaker and which usually takes place in a café. All manner of topics may be discussed but they are very often taken from the arts, politics or philosophy. This is not an entirely Hispanic phenomenon but it is very characteristic.

Tutear – this refers to the use of the second person singular forms of the verb to address someone and can vary in acceptability. Youth and age can affect levels of socially acceptable etiquette as can varying degrees of formality (note that the use of *Usted* can be regarded as overly formal when the conversation has been initiated with *tú*). Mainland Spanish has the additional complication of *vosotros* and some of the Latin American countries, particularly Argentina and Uruguay, that of *vos*.

Common idioms

The standard definition of an idiom is 'a group of words whose meaning cannot be predicted from the meaning of the constituent words' (*Collins English Dictionary*). As with many languages, Spanish has its fair share of these, not to mention a fair share of specialised books on the matter. However, any good dictionary should offer a standard translation of these and many will be rooted in the historical and cultural identity of the language itself.

Many verbs make up idiomatic phrases and the ones most commonly encountered are with the verbs: *dar, echar, estar, hacer, ir, llevar, meter, poner, quedar, ser, tener* and *tomar.*

Dar (to give)

Dar a. To face.
Dar a luz un niño. To give birth.
Dar asco. To disgust.
Dar con. To find/run into.
Dar contra/en. To hit against.
Dar la hora. To strike the hour.

Dar el golpe de gracia.   To finish someone off.

Dar(se) la mano.   To shake hands.

Dar los buenos días.   To say good morning.

Dar gato por liebre.   To sell a pig in a poke/to sell a dud.

Dar guerra.   To cause/make trouble.

Dar la lata.   To make a nuisance of oneself.

Dar por sentado.   To take for granted.

Dar un paseo.   To take a walk/ride.

Dar recuerdos.   To give one's regards/best wishes.

Dar una vuelta.   To go for a short walk/stroll.

Darse la vuelta.   To turn around.

Darse cuenta de.   To realise/be aware of/ take into account.

Darse prisa.   To be in a hurry.

Echar (to throw)

Echar a perder.   To ruin/spoil.

Echar chispas.   To be furious/get angry.

Echar de menos.   To miss.

Echar flores.   To flatter/sweet-talk/butter up.

Echar la bronca a.   To give someone a dressing down/ telling off.

Echar la culpa.   To blame.

Echarse a.   To start to/begin to.

Echárselas de.   To boast of/fancy oneself as.

Estar (to be)

Estar a punto de.   To be about to.

Estar de acuerdo.   To agree.

Estar de buenas.   To be in a good mood.

Estar a sus anchas.   To be comfortable.

Estar como el pez en el agua.   To feel at home.

Estar con el alma en un hilo/en vilo.   To be in suspense/on tenterhooks.

Estar en condiciones.   To be in good shape/be able (to do something).

Estar en la luna/en las nubes.   To have one's head in the clouds/be daydreaming.

Estar fuera de sí.   To be beside oneself (positively and negatively).

Estar hecho polvo.   To be worn out.

Estar hecho una fiera.   To be furious/like a raging bull.

Estar hecho una sopa.   To get soaked.

Estar loco de atar/remate.   To be barking mad.

Estar para chuparse los dedos.   To be delicious.

Estar sin blanca.   To be flat broke/skint.

Hacer (to do/make)

Hacer caso.   To pay attention.

Hacer buenas migas.   To hit it off with someone.

Hacer de las suyas.   To up to one's old tricks.

Hacerse falta.   To need.

Hacer el favor de . . .   Please . . .

Hacer pedazos/añicos.   To smash to bits/tear into pieces.

Hacer un papel.   To play a role.

Hacer juego.   To match.

Hacer la vista gorda.   To turn a blind eye/pretend not to notice.

Hacer época.   To be sensational/attract public attention.

Hacer su agosto.   To make a killing/have a sudden stroke of success.

Hacerse la boca agua.   To make the mouth water.

Hacerse tarde.   To be getting late.

Ir (to go)

Ir al grano.   To go/get straight to the point.

Ir de juerga.   To be out on a spree/out on the town/mucking around.

Ir de mal en peor.   To go from bad to worse.

Ir de marcha.   To go out and enjoy oneself.

Ir sobre ruedas.   To run smoothly.

Ir tirando.   To go smoothly.

Llevar (to carry/take)

Llevar a cabo.   To carry out.

Llevar la contraria.   To contradict.

Llevar leña al monte.   To carry coals to Newcastle/to overdo/to go over the top.

Llevarse como el perro y el gato. To be always arguing/ argue like cat and dog.

Llevarse un chasco. To be disappointed.

Meter (to put)

Meter la pata. To put your foot in your mouth.

Meter las narices. To snoop around/be nosey.

Meterse en la boca del lobo. To enter the lion's den.

Meterse en un callejón sin salida. To get into a difficult situation/fix.

Poner (to put)

Poner a alguien por las nubes. To heap praise on someone/ flatter someone.

Poner pleito. To sue.

Ponérsele a uno la carne de gallina. To get goose bumps.

Ponérsele los cabellos/los pelos de punta. To be terrified/ have one's hair stand on end.

Quedar (to stay/remain)

Quedar boquiabierto. To be left bewildered.

Quedarse con. To keep.

Quedarse con el día y la noche. To be left penniless.

Quedarse de una pieza. To be dumbfounded/speechless.

Quedar en. To agree on.

Quedarse sin blanca. To be flat broke/skint.

Ser (to be)

Ser de buena pasta. To be a nice person/have a good disposition.

Ser de película. To be sensational.

Ser de poca monta. To be of little value.

Ser el colmo. To be the limit.

Ser harina de otro costal/ser otro cantar. To be a horse of a different colour/to be a very different matter.

Ser el ojo derecho. To be someone's pet.

Ser la flor y la nata. To be the best.

Ser pan comido. To be easy as pie.

Ser un cero a la izquierda. To count for nothing/be worthless (person).

Ser un mirlo blanco. To be an impossible dream.

Ser todos oídos. To be all ears.

Ser una lata. To be annoying.

Ser una perla. To be a jewel/treasure.

Ser uña y carne. To be very close (people).

No ser cosa del otro jueves. To be nothing out of the ordinary.

Tener (to have)

Tener ángel/mal ángel. To be charming/lack charm.

Tener buena/mala estrella. To be lucky/unlucky.

Tener éxito. To be successful.

Tener gusto en. To be glad to.

Tener la bondad de. Please .../please be good enough to.

Tener inconveniente. To mind/object to.

Tener la palabra. To have the floor (in order to speak).

Tener los huesos molidos. To be exhausted.

Tener lugar. To take place.

Tener madera para. To be cut out for/made for.

Tener mala cara. To be in a mood/look bad.

Tener malas pulgas. To be irritable/short-tempered.

Tener mundo. To be sophisticated.

Tener ojo de buen cubero. To have a sure/accurate eye.

Tener ojos de lince. To have eyes like a hawk.

Tener pájaros en la cabeza. To have bats in the belfry/be mad/eccentric.

Tener palabra. To keep one's word.

Tener a uno por. To consider someone to be.

No tener donde caerse muerto. Not to have a penny to one's name/to be flat broke/skint.

No tener nombre. To be unspeakable.

No tener pelo de tonto. To be nobody's fool.

No tener pelos en la lengua. To be outspoken.

No tener pies ni cabeza. Not to make any sense/to have no rhyme or reason.

Tener prisa. To be in a hurry.

Tomar (to take)

Tomar a pecho.   To take to heart.
Tomar aliento.   To catch one's breath.
Tomar la palabra.   To take the floor (in order to speak).
Tomar partido por.   To side with.
Tomar la delantera.   To get ahead of.
Tomarle el pelo.   To pull someone's leg/to tease.

Here are some others to whet the appetite:

Andar de boca en boca.   To be generally known.
Andarse por las ramas.   To beat about the bush.
Armarse un escándalo.   To cause a row.
Buscar tres pies al gato.   To split hairs.
No caber en sí/su piel.   To be beside oneself (with joy/anger)/to be presumptuous.
Caerse el alma a los pies.   To be down in the dumps.
Consultar con la almohada.   To sleep on it.
Decirle al oído.   To whisper in someone's ear.
Decirle cuatro verdades.   To tell someone a thing or two.
No decir ni pío.   Not to say a word.
Dejar caer.   To drop.
No dejar piedra por/sin mover.   To leave no stone unturned/try every possible course of action.
Dejar plantado.   To stand someone up/leave someone high and dry/in the lurch.
Dorar la píldora.   To sugar-coat something/to soften the blow.
Dormir a pierna suelta.   To sleep like a log.
Dormir la mona.   To sleep off a hangover.
Faltarle a uno un tornillo.   To have a screw loose/be slightly eccentric, even mad.
Hablar por los codos.   To talk incessantly.
Llamar al pan pan y al vino vino.   To call a spade a spade.
Matar a la gallina de los huevos de oro.   To kill the goose that lays the golden eggs/to destroy a valuable and reliable source of income.
Mandar a freír espárragos.   To tell someone to take a hike.
Matar a dos pájaros de un tiro.   To kill two birds with one stone.

No importar un bledo/un comino/un pepino.   To not give a damn about.

Pasar las de Caín.   To go through hell.

Pedir peras al olmo.   To ask the impossible.

No pegar ojo en toda la noche.   To not sleep a wink.

Quemarse las cejas.   To burn the midnight oil.

No saber a qué carta quedarse.   To be unable to make up one's mind.

Sacar/salir a luz.   To publish.

Sacar en limpio/en claro.   To make clear.

Salirse con la suya.   To get one's own way.

Saltar a la vista.   To be obvious.

Tocar en lo vivo.   To hurt deeply.

Tocar madera.   To touch/knock on wood.

Tragarse la píldora.   To be taken in.

Valer la pena.   To be worthwhile.

Valer un mundo/un ojo de la cara/un Potosí.   To be worth a fortune.

Venir de perlas.   To be just the job.

Verlo todo color de rosa.   To see the world through rose-coloured glasses/to see nothing but good.

Verlo todo negro/a.   To be pessimistic.

No poder verlo ni en pintura.   To not be able to stand the sight of someone.

Volver a las andadas.   To go back to one's old ways.

Volver en sí.   To regain consciousness.

And some others which do not follow on from a verb:

¡A otro perro con ese hueso!   Nonsense!

A pedir de boca.   Smoothly, perfectly.

Como el que más.   As well as/better than anybody else.

Contra viento y marea.   Against all odds.

De buenas a primeras.   At the very beginning/straight away.

De carne y hueso.   Flesh and blood.

De categoría.   Of importance.

Desde que el mundo es el mundo.   Since the world began.

Dicho y hecho.   No sooner said than done.

Dios mediante.   God willing.

El que dirán.   What people say.

Entre la espada y la pared.   Between the Devil and the deep blue sea.

En un abrir y cerrar de ojos.   In a twinkling of an eye.

Está chupado/tirado.   It's a piece of cake.

Hay gato encerrado.   There's something fishy.

Hay moros en la costa.   Be careful./The walls have ears.

Más vale cuatro ojos que dos.   Two heads are better than one.

¡Ojo!   Be careful./Watch out.

Peces gordos.   Big shots/important people/bigwigs.

Sano y salvo.   Safe and sound.

Sin más ni más.   Without further ado.

Trato hecho.   It's a deal.

Sayings and proverbs are also common to many languages and Spanish is no exception, Spanish proverbs representing an idiomatic use of the language. Some common ones are as follows:

A lo hecho, pecho.   It's no use crying over spilt milk.

Al que madruga, Dios le ayuda.   It's the early bird who catches the worm.

Antes de que te cases, mira lo que haces.   Look before you leap.

Dios los cría y ellos se juntan.   Birds of a feather flock together.

El sapo a la sapa la tiene por muy guapa.   Beauty is in the eye of the beholder.

En una hora no se ganó Zamora.   Rome wasn't built in a day.

Eso es el cuento de la lechera/hacer las cuentas de la lechera.   Don't count your chickens before they've hatched.

Los dineros del sacristán, cantando se vienen y cantando se van.   Easy come, easy go.

Más vale pájaro en mano que ciento volando.   A bird in the hand is worth two in the bush./Better the Devil you know.

Obras son amores que no buenas razones.   Actions speak louder than words.

Ojos que no ven, corazón que no siente.   Out of sight, out of mind.

Poderoso caballo es don Dinero.   Money talks.

Quien mala cama hace, en ella se yace.   You made your bed, now lie in it!/Accept the consequences of your own actions.

Sobre gustos no hay nada escrito.   Everyone to his own./ There's no accounting for tastes.

Ver es creer.   Seeing is believing.

Helping you learn

Progress checks

1 Listen out for some of these phrases and try to put them into your own language.
2 Read as often as you can in Spanish and see whether you can spot some idiomatic phrases.
3 Make a note of these phrases and always check their meanings in case there are subtle differences between the English and Spanish versions.

Discussion points

1 At every opportunity, ask a native speaker for an explanation of an idiomatic phrase that you have recently come across but not fully understood.
2 Discuss any difficulties arising from the over-use of literal translation.
3 Do you ever question oddities in your own language?
4 Find out whether fellow students have had the same difficulties when translating idiomatic phrases.

Practical assignments

1 Discuss awkward words and phrases with fellow students.
2 Try to spot which of these words and phrases are used and when.
3 Never miss an opportunity to speak to a native speaker and try out some of your new phrases.

Study tips
1 Speak Spanish at every opportunity.
2 Extend and perfect your Spanish every day.
3 Read something in Spanish every day.
4 Learning a foreign language is a life skill . . . don't give up!

6 The force of "four-letter" words

One-minute overview

Without meaning to be offensive in any way, this is language in its richest form and a word which is everyday in one country may be unspeakable in another . . . with no help to be expected from your average dictionary! *Coger* is a famous case: in Spain it is almost as common as its English equivalent but can be classed as grossly indecent in Argentina and Uruguay. *Pico, polla* and *tirar* are other common danger zones and readers need to be aware of the stares and genuine outrage they might bring upon themselves if they use them unwittingly in certain Spanish-speaking countries! Then there are words which are classed as merely vulgar such as *mear* and those which are somewhat taboo such as *joder* and *coño*, despite their very common usage, especially in Spain.

This chapter aims to give an insight into some of the more commonly used/heard "four-letter" words, their common associations and their associated euphemisms.
The words we are going to give some consideration to are:
cabrón, chucha, coger, cojones, coño, follón, joder, madre, maricón, me cago, mierda, polla, puta and *tirar*, and this list is by no means exhaustive.

Difference of meaning – and ferocity! – of these words in the Spanish-speaking world

Cabrón

Quite possibly one of the strongest and rudest words in the Spanish vocabulary especially if used with the intention to insult! The main English equivalent is 'bastard' or worse. Associated words: *cabronazo* (bastard/bugger) achieves the same level of insult. In Chile the word *cabro* is not quite as forceful and is merely a slang term for 'guy', 'chap', 'fellow' or 'bloke'. *Una cabronada* is a dirty trick played on someone but can also be used to describe unpleasant circumstances in equally unpleasant terms!

Chucha

A word of Amerindian origin, which can vary greatly in both its meaning and usage along with its suggested levels of vulgarity (most of which can be used to refer to the female sexual organs). Quite harmless in other Spanish-speaking countries, any word beginning with '*chu*' is somewhat suspect in and around the Andes. Associated words: *chuchada* in Central America means a 'trick' or 'swindle' and *chuchumeca* in Andean countries means a 'whore'. Not to be confused with the harmless *chucherías*, which are merely children's 'sweeties'!

Coger

A seemingly harmless verb at face value but one which has taken on a vulgar meaning in much of Latin America, particularly in Argentina and Uruguay where the simple original meaning, 'to take', has been mutated to mean 'to fuck', as in to take sexually.

Cojones

A distinctly vulgar term for referring to testicles, perhaps our equivalent of 'balls' or 'bollocks' but somewhat stronger! Related words are *cojonudo*, equally vulgar but very commonly used merely to mean 'terrific', 'fantastic' or 'bloody marvellous'; *una cojudez*, used in the Andean countries and the southernmost part of South America to mean a 'nonsense' or 'stupidity'; and *cojudo*, which refers to a non-castrated animal but, again in the above-mentioned regions, can be used to label someone or something as 'stupid' or 'idiotic'.

Coño

Particularly common in Spain but nevertheless a classic "four-letter" word. Its true meaning (vulgar reference to the female sexual organs) is much more offensive in female company than its intended everyday usage which amounts to a fairly harmless exclamation of surprise equivalent to, if only a little stronger than, *¡hombre!* (see page 76). Outside Spain the word is much less used, if at all, except perhaps in and around Mexico and Venezuela, or in Chile where it is used as a slang word for 'Spaniard' (probably because of the Spaniards' over-use of it!). Associated words: *coñazo*, which merely relates to the equivalent of something or someone being a 'pain', and *coña*, which quite innocently refers to someone joking around (*estar de coña*) or at most 'taking the piss'. A euphemistic usage I noted in and around Madrid was *coñi* so as perhaps not to offend any sensitive female present at the time!

Follón

A fairly harmless word on the whole despite the force of its origin (*follar* is 'to fuck'), it merely refers to things being in a state, a mess or generally not quite under control (similar to *jaleo*) and *un follón* is often used with the verb *tener* or *armar* (meaning 'to kick up a fuss'). Associated words: *follonero/a* is some sort of troublemaker and *follon(e)arse* in and around Mexico means 'to pass wind/to fart silently'!

Joder

The one you have been waiting for because you have probably heard it the most often! It is one of the coarsest words in the language and equates with 'to fuck' in English. Likewise it is used in a multitude of contexts which generally refer to messing someone or something around, or generally 'screwing up'. In and around Chile it has become widely used with the latter meaning, and in Spain it is the ultimate of swear words but used with the regularity of such words as *¡hombre!* It is best avoided in and around Mexico as they have their own equivalent (*chingar*). Associated words: *joda*, a 'joke' or a 'bloody nuisance'; *jodido*, as an adjective, 'bloody awkward/difficult', 'buggered' or 'pissed off'; and *jodienda* means that something is a 'fucking nuisance'. Euphemisms I heard in and around Madrid were *jo* and *jope*.

Madre

Perhaps one that you were not expecting to see on the hit list of swear words but insults connected with mothers are very common (see also *puta* below), so much so that in much of Latin America the word is avoided where possible and, for references to family members, *mamá* and *papá* are used in preference as are *abuelita* and *abuelito* in preference to *abuela* and *abuelo*. In and around Mexico the phrase *¡Tu abuela!* is the equivalent of the exclamation 'Balls!'

Maricón

Normally translated as 'queer' (the female equivalent for 'lesbian' being *una tortillera*) but also representing the height of pejorative insult and not one to be used lightly, especially in mixed company. *Marica* is also used but is a little less forceful. Associated words: *mariconada* means a 'dirty trick'; *mariconeo* refers to homosexual activities; *mariconera* means 'a handbag used by men'; and *mariconear* means 'to poof around'.

Me cago

From the verb *cagar*, the equivalent of which is 'to shit', this expression is relatively harmless in the swing of things and equates to a mere expression of contempt: *Me cago en* . . . is not much more than 'Bugger that!' or 'Sod that!' There is a euphemistic version which comes out as *¡Mecachis!* and is merely softer on the ear! Related words are *cagado* ('shit-scared') and *cagón/-a* ('coward').

Mierda

Probably the safest swear word for an adventurous foreigner to use but I would still err on the side of caution. It is the equivalent of 'shit' and a euphemism I heard in Madrid was the word *miércoles* ('Wednesday'!); I took this to be the equivalent of our use of 'Oh, sugar!' so as not to offend!

Polla

Normally taken to mean a 'female chicken/hen', it is to be avoided if possible in Spain as it is a commonly vulgar term for the male sexual organ. Associated words: *pollastro/pollastrón* mean a 'sly fellow' and *pollo*, in Mexico, is a would-be immigrant to the USA.

Puta

Unfortunately widely used to insult as *puta* means 'whore' and the derogatory Spanish phrase *hijo de puta* is a lot stronger than the English 'son-of-a-bitch'. However, I do not consider 'whore' as a completely satisfactory translation as it implies a professional who is paid for her services. In the Hispanic world, *puta* can be attributed to any female who has sex outside marriage and therefore the word is much closer to our insult of 'hussy/slag/slut/slapper'. Associated words: *putada* means a 'dirty trick/bloody shame'; *puteada*, in Latin America, is a shower of gross insults; *putear* means 'to bugger about/muck around'; *putería* refers to 'womanly wiles/a brothel/the activities of prostitution'; *puto*, as an adjective, means 'bloody awful' and, as a noun, a 'male prostitute'.

Tirar(se)

Tirar normally means 'to throw away' or 'to shoot' but this word has gone astray in the same way as *coger* (see above) has in Andean countries.

Quite obviously there are many more "four-letter" words in existence in everyday Spanish and what I have aimed to do here is to highlight some of the more common ones. Also, at this point, I would like to draw the reader's attention to the fact that using such words in any language does not show a level of mastery of that particular language, but rather knowing when not to use them or being fully aware of their implication in any given situation shows a much more cultured approach overall.

Helping you learn

Progress checks

1 List different ways of saying the same thing and check their meaning.
2 Write down subtleties discussed and check your understanding of them with fellow students
3 When listening to native speakers talk, concentrate on the usage of "four-letter" words.

Discussion points

1 Share your experiences of Spanish "four-letter" words with fellow students.
2 Know which expression to use and when to use it.
3 How important is it to be aware of subtleties of expression in a language to avoid causing offence?
4 Discuss the difficulties arising from someone's over-use of four-letter words in an attempt to be one of the crowd.

Practical assignments

1 Discuss any problems in the use of frank language with fellow students.
2 Try to spot which Spanish four-letter words are used and when, and the degree of force intended.
3 Listen to everyday conversational Spanish as often as you can and pick out examples of four-letter words and the context in which they are used.

Study tips

1 If you are given the chance to speak to, or stay with, a Spanish family, welcome it with open arms.
2 Speak Spanish at every opportunity and practise what you know but be very careful not to swear like a trooper every time you open your mouth!
3 Think in Spanish every day.
4 Learning a foreign language is a skill for life . . . but so is knowing how to use it appropriately.
5 Never give up and always remember that practice makes perfect.

Using Spanish correctly and with fluency

One-minute overview

Every student of any foreign language dreams of speaking that language 'like a native' and indeed some people do achieve this. However, every language has its own peculiarities and some of these will be discussed in this chapter as separate issues from any of those discussed previously, yet bearing in mind that they will have an impact ultimately on everything that has gone before.

The points I wish to touch upon in this chapter are:
- pronunciation in general
- the purity of vowels
- the pronunciation of certain consonants
- use of the written accent
- use of the diminutive
- double and final consonants
- intonation
- Latin American usage
- unspoken fluency

Pronunciation in general

I am fully aware that all exam board criteria have, at some point, a phrase which states 'can reasonably be understood by a sympathetic native speaker', or words to that effect. However, I am also fully in favour of at least trying to get the pronunciation of any language as correct as possible and thus showing an admiration and appreciation of the beauty of the language in question. The gift of mimicry is not one that we all have (and perhaps even less so as we all advance in years!) but it certainly represents a good place to start, as does having a 'good ear' or at least the willingness or ability to listen attentively. Previous chapters have given you an insight into the subtleties, and indeed some of the crudities, of spoken Spanish and an awareness of these aspects and their respective hazards is also a valuable tool when trying to speak a language *con soltura* (fluently).

The purity of vowels

The vowels in Spanish are pure, which means that they are always pronounced in an unvarying way. They are short and precise and do not have the wide-ranging variety of those of the English language (a set of twelve phonemes/distinct sounds for the five vowels of the alphabet). Knowing this and making a regular (albeit on the quiet) attempt to practise pronouncing A-E-I-O-U whenever you can, should enforce a distinctly more precise and crisp pronunciation of any word in the Spanish language. Note: the vowel 'u' is mute in the combinations 'gue' (*guerra*), 'gui' (*guitarra*), 'que' (*quemadura*), 'qui' (*esquiar*). If the 'u' is to be pronounced in the combinations 'gue' or 'gui' then it should carry a diaeresis: *agüero/lingüística*.

When diphthongs (two vowels together to make one syllable) or triphthongs (three vowels in the same syllable) occur, each vowel should retain its original sound in Spanish: *hueso/deuda/Europa/Uruguay/miau*.

The pronunciation of certain consonants

'B' vs 'V'

Very few native speakers differentiate clearly between these two consonants, which can lead to a whole host of problems, the main ones being linked to the spelling of unfamiliar words heard for the first time – by native and non-native speakers alike! A fairly sound approach to this problem is to read widely and thus familiarise yourself with words at every opportunity. We can also resort to mimicry: trying to imitate a word is a far better way of attempting to say it correctly than tracing it back to its written form. Also, there is nothing wrong in asking the person in question: '*¿Con b ó con v?*'

'C', 'S' and 'Z'

These letters are involved in the previously mentioned difference between *seseando* and *ceceando* (see p. 88). A very strong characteristic of spoken peninsular Spanish, especially in more central and northern regions, is the way in which 'z' is pronounced in any context and how 'c' is pronounced when followed by either 'e' or 'i'. The pronunciation is like the English 'th' in the word *think*. However, this is not the case in Andalucía (southern Spain) and the Canary Islands nor, in fact, in the rest of the Spanish-speaking world where both consonants would be pronounced as if they were a letter 's'.

'CH'

In the Spanish alphabet this is considered as a separate letter because it represents a single sound and is not a combination of other sounds. It is pronounced like the English 'ch' in *child*.

'H'

This letter is completely mute in Spanish and should never be pronounced.

'J' and 'G'

The consonant 'j' and the combinations 'ge' and 'gi' are pronounced in a similar way to the ending of the Scottish word *loch*. It is a markedly stronger sound in certain regions of Spain and Latin America but much softer in Caribbean regions, where it is like an English 'h' as in the word *hello*. When the consonant 'g' is followed by 'a', 'o' or 'u', the 'g' sound is much more like the English 'g' in words such as *girl guide/gossip/gas*.

'LL' and 'Y'

The important thing to remember here is that 'll' is never pronounced in the English way. It is considered as a separate letter of the alphabet (as it represents a separate sound) and, although it is pronounced slightly more strongly at the beginning of a word, the pronunciation of both 'll' and the consonant 'y' are different depending upon the variety of Spanish spoken.

'Ñ'

This is another of the Spanish consonants considered as a separate letter of the alphabet because it represents an individual sound. However, it does not appear in the English language and the nearest sound to it is somewhere around the sound of 'gn' in words such as *poignancy*. When speaking and writing, it is very important to make a clear distinction between 'n' and 'ñ' because if you do not the whole meaning of a word can change!

Compare: *cana* (grey hair) with *caña* (a small glass of beer), or *mano* (hand) with *maño* (adjective or noun for 'Aragonese').

'R' and 'RR'

Again, these are considered to be separate letters of the Spanish alphabet because they represent individual sounds. When in the middle of a word, the letter 'r' is pronounced more softly. When at the beginning of a word, or doubled, it is rolled and the pronunciation is much harsher. The letter 'rr' is never placed at the beginning of a word itself. In certain parts of Latin America, and when 'r' occurs in combinations such as 'tr' and 'dr', the pronunciation changes again and becomes almost like that of the letter 's' in the English word *television*.

'X'

In English, we have a soft (as in *exempt*) and a harsh (as in *excitement*) pronunciation of this letter and the Spanish pronunciation is generally much closer to the latter. However, in Spain and in some parts of Latin America it can also be pronounced like an 's' before the majority of consonants. Please note that there are a few exceptions to this where 'x' will sound like the consonant 'j' and can even be exchanged for that same letter: *Javier* and *Xavier*. This can also be found in some Latin American place names, particularly in *Mexico/Méjico/México*, as their roots are in the native American languages.

The use of the written accent

Unlike English, Spanish is very evenly accentuated, and when spoken well, has very little heavy accentuation. If stress is needed on a particular point, Spanish speakers will not change the emphasis of the word itself as English speakers do, but rather add something to the sentence to enhance the meaning. Very often, using the personal pronoun is one way of emphasising what is being said:

I say.   *Digo.*

I say.   Digo *yo.*

You will also come across the addition of useful little words such as *lo, ni, que* and *ya* (see page 77); the use of words and expressions which are more commonly found in written work, such as *en cambio*; and the use of *sí* and *no* to emphasise a contrasting idea:

Para tí sí, para mí no.   For you maybe but not for me.

Hasta or *incluso* can also be used to express surprise at something:

¡Han debido haber hasta cien!   There must have been at least a hundred of them!

The way a word is accentuated is also commonly referred to as 'stress', meaning the emphasis which is put on any particular syllable of the word in question. As in English, it is very important that a word is stressed correctly because otherwise, once again, we could be faced with a very wrong rendition!

Compare: m**i**nute (measurement of time) with min**u**te (tiny) and, more so perhaps when writing in Spanish, *este* with *éste* and *esté* (demonstrative adjective with demonstrative pronoun and present subjunctive of the verb *estar*!)

The general rules for the correct use of a **written accent** in Spanish are fairly straightforward and, if an accent is used, it will always be written over a stressed vowel:

– words which end in a vowel or the consonants 'n' or 's' are stressed on the penultimate syllable and carry no written accent;

– words which end in a consonant (except 'n' or 's') are stressed on the last syllable and carry no written accent.

Any other words which do not fit into these first two categories will usually be one of the following and will usually carry a written accent:

– to distinguish two words with different meanings, such as *si* (if) and *sí* (yes)

– to distinguish a question word from a relative pronoun *¿cuándo?* (when?), *¿dónde?* (where?), *¿por qué?* (why), *¿qué?* (what?), *¿quién?* (who?)

– when words end with a stressed vowel, such as *¡ojalá!* (if only!)

– when words have preterite and future verb endings and the second person plural of present tense endings, some of which carry written accents

– when words end in combinations with 'ión', 'ón', 'án', 'én' or 'és'. Note, however, that such words will lose the accent if put into their feminine or plural forms as they then follow the usual rules obediently:
inglés goes to *inglesa* or *ingleses*

– when words are stressed on the penultimate syllable even if they end in a consonant and will therefore carry a written accent to indicate their exception to the general rule:
fácil/difícil

– when words have an object pronoun attached to the end:
Dígame/dáselo/¿por qué estás *haciéndolo* así?

– when words contain a letter 'i' that needs to be separated from another vowel:
zapatería/frutería and imperfect verb endings.

Use of the diminutive

This is another way of emphasising a particular word for a particular reason or purpose. Attaching 'ito/ita' to the end of an adjective can personalise a word instantly and not just make its meaning 'smaller'.

Note: *Espere un momento* and *Espere un momentito*; both mean 'Hang on a minute' but the latter is a touch more friendly.

The diminutive is also a neat way of dealing with words such as 'rather' and 'somewhat' and the extremely English use of '-ish':

Pronto (soon).   *Prontito* (fairly soon).

Cerca (near).   *Cerquita* (quite near/not very far at all).

Rosa (pink).   *De color rosita* (pinkish).

One very common adjective meaning 'small' can also have a diminutive form:

Chico (small).   *Chiquitito* (teeny/tiny/minute).

Double and final consonants

Spanish is not over-fond of using double consonants, especially 's', and will often have a word spelt with an even distribution of vowels either to keep the consonants apart or to make them manageable in some other way. A prime example of this is when Spaniards generally try to pronounce the English combination of 'sp' and inadvertently add a vowel to make the pronunciation easier for them: 'E-spain' and 'e-special' are often heard. Another nightmare for native Spanish speakers is pronouncing three or more consonants together in English: imagine their heartache when they are asked to read aloud 'twelfth', 'eighth' and, worst of all, 'crisps'!

Final consonants are not always the flavour of the month either, particularly if originating from a foreign word, but ones which naturally occur in Spanish itself are tolerated (such as l, n , r, s and z). However, final d's tend to get ignored, which I soon discovered while living in *Madrí*.

Intonation

One of the most important things to master in any language, albeit sometimes one of the hardest, is a natural-sounding intonation. Sometimes you are more likely to be understood if your intonation sounds authentic and some of your vocabulary a bit suspect than vice versa. So we are back to good old-fashioned mimicry at its best.

Latin American usage

All countries have their distinct regionalisms and different countries speaking the same language will undoubtedly have made their own mark upon it over time. A prime example of this is the different accents and, indeed, vocabulary used among speakers of English from various parts of the British Isles, from the United States, Canada, Australia, New Zealand and so on. Such is the case with Spanish: spoken in at least 21 countries worldwide as a first language and several more as a second.

When teaching Spanish, a good teacher should endeavour to point out these differences to their students while stressing that no version is 'purer' than another. The main noticeable difference between peninsular Spanish (spoken north of Andalucía) and that spoken in Latin America and Andalucía is the pronunciation of 'z' and 'c' (when they come before 'e' or 'i'): they are like an 's' in the latter case as opposed to 'th' in the former. Apart from anything else, this difference can lead to endless spelling mistakes and possible confusion, with *tres* sounding like *trece* and so on! There is also the problem of the clear lack of distinction between 'll' and 'y', and the extending of vowels, which is strictly non-peninsular: *l-e-e-e-jos* rather than *lejísimo*.

Apart from this, a few cases of dropped 's' and a smattering of vocabulary variance, it is one and the same language and, as with any language, it is constantly changing wherever it is spoken. Learners are there to appreciate and adapt to change and wonder at the richness of the language they endeavour to master.

Years of studying Spanish do not fully prepare you for the linguistic or cultural experience that is Latin America, where indigenous languages are still widely used in many areas, even though Spanish is the official language in most South American countries. In UK schools, Castilian Spanish is most often taught, so for those of us who have spent years studying it, such an imposing linguistic diversity is bound to leave us somewhat bemused and bewildered.

Nevertheless, you would expect to feel confident enough to order a meal but this is one such linguistic area that could potentially lead to a lot of confusion, with words which look familiar but meanings which are not, even within the Peninsula itself.

Una marinera may be understood by a Valencian to be a 'seafood paella' but someone from the region of Murcia would expect to see an oval-shaped breadstick topped with potato salad and an anchovy! In Paraguay, *surubí* and *ensalada de palta* may be vaguely recognisable to a Hispanist but not necessarily as a fish dish with avocado salad. In a similar vein, *cuy*, which is a local delicacy in Cuzco, would perhaps not be readily chosen for its cultural appeal once you have been made aware that it actually refers to an undoubtedly succulent guinea-pig! What is happening here from a linguistic point of view is that, as with many foods and local delicacies all over the world, local terms are used to name many items of local produce which might not be eaten in neighbouring areas or even known in surrounding countries.

Unspoken fluency

By this I am referring to a Spaniard's use of body language and gesture. Worth a mention as they represent yet another level of fluency which is sometimes difficult for a non-native speaker to achieve. Again, we revert to mimicry because to imitate on a regular basis is a sure way of adapting to this unspoken part of any language. There are a lot of these gestures in everyday usage and here I would just like to point out some of the more common ones:

1 Putting the index finger against one's lips, I think, is fairly international to indicate that the speaker requires silence.

2 Clicking of the fingers, used in the Spanish-speaking world to indicate to someone that they get on and do what they have been asked, and quickly!

3 Joining the first finger and thumb, kissing them and then pulling the fingers away to indicate sheer delight or satisfaction with something (eg wine or food).

4 Using the index finger to pull down the skin under the eye ever so slightly to indicate to someone that they should watch out/be aware that the person they may be talking about is within earshot/to call their attention to something. This can be accompanied by the exclamation *¡Ojo!*

5 Gently tapping one's cheek to indicate that someone has a bit of a cheek/is being a bit fresh.

6 Clicking one's fingers to get attention, for example in a restaurant, is perfectly acceptable in the Spanish-speaking world.

7 Appearing to wipe one's hand across one's thigh indicates that you consider a particular person to be overdoing it with praise for someone else/sucking up to someone/generally being too familiar.

8 Again, a fairly internationally obscene gesture, that of a clenched fist with a raised middle finger to indicate distaste, disgust or general disrespect.

9 There is also the very common twist/flick of the wrist (as if dancing a *sevillana*!) used to indicate some sort of exaggeration.

10 The waving of the index finger from side to side to show that what someone is saying is incorrect or that you disagree.

Helping you learn

Progress checks

1 Write down explanations for different pronunciations of the same word and check your answers.
2 List different ways of saying the same thing and check their meaning.

Discussion points

1 Do you agree that the vast amount of variation within the English language must give foreigners a hard time?
2 Accept the rules which help you to learn to speak a foreign language better . . . that is what they are there for!
3 Discuss difficulties encountered by fellow students.

Practical assignments

1 Never miss the opportunity to visit a Spanish-speaking country and savour the richness of the language at source.
2 Listen to Spanish TV and radio whenever possible.

Study tips

1 Never give up when confronted with the difficulties covered in this book.
2 Do not worry when things do not fall into place straight away.
3 Everyone goes through the same experience.
4 The only secret is practice.

8 Mastering difficult structures

One-minute overview

In this final chapter, students of mine, both past and present, will not be surprised to find that the content is heavily grammatical . . . for which I make no apologies! I aim to give an insight into not only being confident about fluency when speaking Spanish, but also being grammatically correct at the same time. There are certain tricks to learning to speak a foreign language and many have already been discussed in previous chapters (mimicry being the most prevalent). However, to speak a language well is one thing but to speak it with accuracy is a whole different ball game and here are the points to be considered in this section:

- the use of personal *a*
- the use of *ahora bien*
- the use of the article
- the use of adjectives
- the use of collective nouns
- the use of impersonal verbs
- the importance of sentence structure
- the use of the subjunctive mood
- the use of prepositions and their associated verbs
- specific translation pitfalls

The use of personal *a*

This is a grammatical concept which is particular to the Spanish language and for which there is no English equivalent. To get a little bit technical: when the direct object of the verb is a person or persons, the preposition *a* needs to be popped between it and the verb:

Quiero mucho a mi madre.   I love my mother very much.

It is not used with objects or things but can be used with pets (to which we are emotionally attached):

Mi hija adora a su gato. My daughter adores her (pet) cat.

Note: the verb *tener* does not take the personal *a*:

Tengo dos hermanos. I have (got) two brothers.

The use of *ahora bien*

Ahora bien is a pragmatic device, particularly when speaking in Spanish, which signals that a new point is being made which relates, nevertheless, to what has already gone before. It is therefore signalling that the point which has just been made is about to be reinforced or backed up in some way:

No me gustó lo que hiciste, *ahora bien* si te disculpas me lo pensaré de nuevo. I didn't like what you did *but* if you apologise, I may reconsider.

The use of the articles

There are three articles in Spanish, the **definite** ('the') and the **indefinite** ('a/an/some/a few/a couple of'), each one with four variants, and the single **neuter** form.

Definite. *El/la/los/las.*

Indefinite. *Un/una/unos/unas.*

Neuter. *Lo.*

The definite article

The definite article agrees in number and gender with the noun it is modifying. However, if a feminine singular noun begins with a stressed *a* or *ha* then *el* is used instead of *la*:

El hambre. Hunger.

El agua. Water.

El hacha. Axe.

Note, however, that if the definite article is before an adjective which is itself before a noun, then the above point is not observed:

En la ardiente oscuridad. In the burning darkness.

La alta montaña. The high mountain.

There is also something which happens to the masculine singular definite article when preceded by *a* or *de*. This is called 'contraction' and it occurs as follows:

A + EL = AL

DE + EL = DEL

Voy al banco los lunes.   I go to the bank on Mondays.

Este paquete viene del consulado.   This packet has come from the consulate.

This contraction does not happen when the definite article *el* is part of a name or title:

Las obras de El Greco[3]

The definite article **is** used in certain situations or to perform certain functions within a sentence:

– before every noun even when there are several in a list (this is not always a feature of English)
Tengo la maleta, el pasaporte y la cámara conmigo.   I have the suitcase, passport and camera with me.

– with a noun when making a general statement
No me gusta el café.   I don't like coffee.

– with a noun denoting weight/measure
5€ el kilo.   5€ per kilo.

– before a noun which indicates a profession/rank/title followed by the name of the person:
El Señor López es un hombre muy inteligente.   Mr López is a very intelligent man.
El catedrático de inglés es mi tío.   The English professor/lecturer is my uncle.

This does not happen, however, when addressing the person directly:
Buenas noches, Señor López.   Good evening, Mr López.

– with the name of a subject matter:
Estudio la geografía.   I study geography.

---

[3] Reproduced from Phil Turk and Mike Zollo, *(ibid)*

Note, however, that this is optional if the subject matter is a **language** and particularly after the verb *hablar* and after the prepositions *de* and *en*. It is also commonly omitted after the verbs *aprender, enseñar, estudiar, leer, practicar* and *saber*:

Hablo español con soltura.   I speak Spanish fluently.

Me encanta cuando me hablas en francés.   I love it when you speak to me in French.

Llevo muchos años aprendiendo/enseñando italiano.   I have been learning/teaching Italian for many years.

– with the days of the week (in English we say 'on'):

El lunes/los lunes.   On Monday/on Mondays.

Note, however, that the definite article is not used after the verb *ser*:

Hoy es lunes.   Today is Monday.

– with parts of the body and articles of clothing, especially if the owner is clearly stated and if a reflexive verb is being used:

Me duele el brazo.   My arm is hurting me.

Voy a ponerme la falda roja.   I'm going to put on my red skirt.

– with the seasons of the year:

En la primavera/el verano/el otoño/el invierno.   In the spring/summer/autumn/winter.

However, it can be omitted after the preposition *en* when the event in question occurs in that season on a regular basis:

Siempre va a España en invierno.   He always goes to Spain in the winter.

To show possession with the preposition *de* + noun:

El coche del Americano.   The American man's car.

La iglesia del barrio.   The local church.

Note, however, that this does not happen when a proper noun is used:

El bolígrafo de Mariano.   Mariano's pen.

– with the names of some cities/countries/continents, although this tendency is generally dying out in modern spoken language. The definite article must be used, however, if the name of the country in question is modified in any way:

la Argentina, el Brasil, el Canadá, los Estados Unidos, la Habana, la América del Norte, la América Central, la América del Sur, el Perú, el Japón.

En la España demócrata de hoy.   In democratic Spain of today.

Las reuniones se celebran en la Europa central.   The meetings are taking place in central Europe.

– with the names of rivers, oceans and mountains:
El Támesis es el río famoso de Londres.   The Thames is London's famous river.

Me gusta esquiar en los Pirineos.   I like to ski/go skiing in the Pyrenees.

– with a proper noun modified by an adjective:
La pequeña María.   Little Maria.

– with a noun preceded by a preposition:
Nosotros los ingleses.   We English.

– with an infinitive when used as a noun and particularly when so at the beginning of a sentence:
El trabajar demasiado no es bueno.   Working too much is not a good thing.

Note there are some exceptions, mainly to be found in proverbial phrases (see previous listings) page 96 and not usually used with an infinitive if it does not begin the sentence.

– when telling the time:
Es la una y media.   It's half past one.
Son las cuatro.   It's four o'clock.
Note, however:
Es mediodía/medianoche.   It's midday/midnight.

– in some set phrases in Spanish but whose equivalent in English does not always require it:
A/en/de la iglesia.   To/in/from (the) church.
En la televisión.   On TV.
En el mar.   At sea, on/in the sea.

The definite article is **not** used:

– when a noun is preceded by another noun (in apposition):
París, capital francesa del amor. Paris, the French capital city of love.

– with a numeral that denotes the order of succession of a monarch:
Felipe II. Philip the Second.

– before a mass/count noun which only refers to an unspecified quantity of the whole:
María compró pescado. Maria bought fish (but not every piece in the shop).
Mi madre tiene paciencia. My mother is patient (most of the time).
Si te duele la cabeza, toma aspirinas. If you have a headache, take aspirin (but not the whole bottle/box).

– usually after *haber*:
Hay gente por las calles. There are people on the streets.

– when two nouns are joined by the preposition *de* to form a compound noun, the definite article is omitted before the *second* noun:
El dolor de estómago. Stomach-ache.
Los libros de texto. Textbooks.

– in many adverbial phrases in Spanish whose English equivalents **do** take a definite article
A nombre de. In the name of.
Estoy en camino. I am on the way.
A corto/largo plazo. In the short/long run.

The indefinite article
The indefinite article also agrees in gender and number with the noun it is modifying and, when used in its plural form, indicates an indefinite number:
Unas veinte personas. Some twenty people/about twenty people.

Like its definite counterpart, the indefinite article **is** used in certain situations and with certain specific functions within a sentence:

– when you want to say 'a/an' or to use the numeral 'one':
Un coche.   A car/one car.
Note: to clarify that you mean 'one' as opposed to 'a/an', the word *solamente* is very useful:
Solamente un coche.   (only) One car.

– with a noun of nationality/profession/rank/religion which has already been modified with an adjective:
El Señor López es un profesor excelente.   Mr López is an excellent teacher.
Note, however, that this is not the case when just stating someone's nationality/profession/rank/religion per se:
El Señor López es profesor.   Mr López is a teacher.

– before each noun in a series (which we do not tend to do in English)
Tengo una falda, un jersey y unos zapatos en la mochila. I have a skirt, jumper and (some) shoes in my rucksack.

The indefinite article is **not** used:

– before *cien* and *mil*:
Me costó cien libras.   It cost me a/one hundred pounds.
Te lo he dicho mil veces.   I've told you a thousand times.

– with *cierto/a, tal, otro/a, medio*:
Anda con cierta persona.   He is out with a certain person.
Tal caso.   Such a case.
En otro momento.   At another time.
Media docena.   Half a dozen.

– when used with the exclamation *¡qué!*:
¡Qué cosa más rara!   What a strange thing!
(See page 78 for more examples.)

– after *ser* (to be) or *hacerse* (to become) with professions, occupations, nationality, religion, social status or gender:

Quiero ser profesora.   I want to be a teacher.
Después de muchos años de estudios se hizo profesora.   After many years of study she became a teacher.
Soy católica.   I am Catholic.
Note, however, if the noun is modified by a phrase or adjective, then the indefinite article *is* necessary:
Soy una católica practicante.   I am a practising Catholic.
Es una profesora simpática.   She is a nice teacher.

– when implying 'some' before a singular noun, there is no need to use anything (if you are familiar with French, there is no equivalent of 'du/de la'):
¿Quieres café?   Do you want (some) coffee?
Para mí, voy a tomar pollo asado.   I am going to have (the/some) roast chicken.

– after *no hay* or *no tener*:
Fui al mercado tarde y ya no había gangas.   I went to the market late and there were no bargains (left).
No tengo papel para apuntar el número.   I have no paper to note down the number.

– usually after certain verbs (*tener, llevar, usar, comprar, buscar, sacar*):
Busco casa que tenga jardín.   I am looking for a house with a garden.
Vete al mercado y compra fruta.   Go to the market and buy some fruit.
Lleva corbata.   He is wearing a tie.

– when nouns are plural, a fairly reliable rule of thumb is: when we use nothing or say 'any' in English, use nothing in Spanish, and when we mean 'some' in English use *unos/unas* in Spanish:
¿Tiene helado?   Do you have any ice-cream?
¿Tiene helados variados?   Do you have various ice-creams?
¿Quieres bombones?   Do you want sweets?
Vamos a tomar unos helados.   Let's get some ice-creams.
¿Quieres unos bombones?   Do you want some/a few sweets?

The neuter article

The neuter article, *lo*, has mainly idiomatic uses and generally speaking it is used:

– with a masculine singular form of an adjective when used as a noun:
lo bueno es que/lo malo es que/lo peor.   The good thing is/the bad thing is/the worst thing.

– with a past participle:
lo dicho.   What has been said.

– with an adjective/adverb + *que* when used to mean 'how':
Ahora entiendo lo difícil que es.   Now I know how difficult it is.

The use of adjectives

An adjective is a word used to describe a noun or pronoun. An adjective agrees with the gender and number of what it is describing. Positioning an adjective within a sentence is very important as it can, in some cases, change the meaning of what you wish to say. In addition, there are some adjectives which, despite working to describe something, are used in a different grammatical way in Spanish.

Agreement

As previously stated, an adjective agrees in gender and number with whatever it is describing. An adjective that ends in *-o* in its masculine singular form, will very often have a corresponding feminine singular form ending in *-a* and corresponding plural forms ending in *-os* and *-as*: *rojo/roja/rojos/rojas*.

An adjective which ends in a consonant or the letter *-e* does not generally have a feminine form unless it is an adjective of nationality or one which ends in one of the following combinations: *-án*, *-ón*, *-ín*, or *-or*:
Un chico formal/una chica formal.   A well-behaved boy/girl.
Mandón/mandona.   Bossy.
Español/española.   Spanish.

When an adjective ends in a consonant, add -*es* to form the plural (note previous notes on accentuation on p. 109/10).

Inglés/ingleses.

Joven/jóvenes.

Difícil/difíciles.

If an adjective is describing two or more masculine nouns, the masculine plural form is used; if an adjective is describing two or more feminine nouns, the feminine plural form is used. However, if an adjective is describing two or more nouns of different genders then note that it is the masculine plural form which will override:

Tengo un gato y un perro, ambos son negros.   I have a cat and a dog; both are black.

Mis dos hermanas son rubias.   My two sisters are blonde.

Mi padre y mi madre son británicos.   My father and my mother are British.

Positioning

In most instances, an adjective is placed after the noun it is modifying or describing. However, there is a certain small group of adjectives which can come before a noun and when they do, their meaning changes. Adjectives in this category are *viejo*, *pobre*, *nuevo* and *grande*:

Un *viejo* amigo.   An *old* friend (one you have known for a long time).

Un amigo *viejo*.   An *old* friend (of advanced years).

Una mujer *pobre*.   A *poor* woman (with no money).

Una *pobre* mujer.   A *poor* woman (in a sad state).

Un *nuevo* sombrero.   A *new* hat (different from the one before).

Un sombrero *nuevo*.   A *new* hat (brand new).

Un edificio *grande*.   A *big* building (large/tall).

Un *gran* edificio.   A *great/magnificent* building.

The last example also shows us how *apocopation* works. This occurs when a shorter form of some adjectives is used. It commonly takes place only in the masculine singular form of the adjective and, again, when it is placed before the noun it is describing. Apocopation also occurs with *bueno*, *malo*, *primero*, *tercero*, *alguno*, *ninguno*, *uno* and *Santo*:

Hace *buen/mal* tiempo.   The weather is *good/bad*.

Está en el *primer/tercer* piso.   It is on the *first/third* floor.

¿Habrá *algún* problema con esta idea?   Is there *some* problem with this idea?

No, no hay *ningún* problema.   No, there is *no* problem.

San Sebastián.   *St.* Sebastian, but note (due to pronunciation quirks) Santo Tomás/Santo Domingo.

Note also, going back to the word *grande*, that this will shorten to *gran* when it precedes any singular noun, whether masculine or feminine.

In addition, *ciento* will shorten to *cien* before any plural noun, whether masculine or feminine, except in the numbers 101 through to 199:

Cien niños.   One/a hundred boys.

Cien niñas.   One/a hundred girls.

Ciento ochenta.   180.

And last, but by no means least, *cualquiera/cualesquiera* lose their final -*a* when placed before a noun:

No lo diría a *cualquier* hombre.   I wouldn't say it to just *any* man.

Other adjectival uses

To say what something is made of in Spanish, the construction **de** + **noun** is needed and works in place of the adjective itself:

Una bolsa de plástico.   A plastic bag.

Una chaqueta de cuero.   A leather jacket.

Una corbata de seda.   A silk tie.

In English we quite happily use another noun in place of an adjective (tennis match) but this is not correct in Spanish and once again the construction **de** + **noun** is used as a substitute:

Un partido de tenis.   A tennis match.

El tren de Madrid.   The Madrid train.

Lo + adjective

A common phrase with the meaning 'the — part/thing/bit':

Lo bueno es que . . .   The good thing is . . .

Dime lo importante.   Tell me the important part.

Y cuando llegó a lo interesante . . .   And when it got to the interesting bit . . .

Anaphora/cataphora

Anaphora is the use of a word/words which has/have no meaning of its/their own but which acquires a meaning from a previous context and avoids lexical repetition:

Los mismos/las mismas.   The same (ones).

En dicha reunión.   In the aforementioned meeting.

Cataphora, or forward anaphora, deals with what is about to be stated:

Lo veremos de inmediato.   We shall soon see.

Ellipsis

This is when part of a sentence, essential for its overall meaning, is omitted. It is used for economy or emphasis of style:

Tras la recepción, en los jardines del hotel Reina Sofía.   *After the reception, in the gardens of the Reina Sofia hotel.*

Here the verb has been completely elided/omitted, the usage is adjectival and although commonly used in spoken language, it is not considered to be correct or good style when written.[4]

The use of collective nouns

As defined in *Collins English Dictionary*, a collective noun is 'a noun that is singular in form but that refers to a group of people or things'. Collective nouns are usually used with a singular verb but, in British usage, a plural verb can be used where reference is being made to a collection of individual objects or persons rather than to the group as a

---

[4] Leo Hickey, former lecturer at Salford University

unit. However, it is **not** good style when the same collective noun is treated as both singular and plural within the same sentence.

Some common collective nouns in Spanish:
El profesorado.　　The teaching profession.
Voy a comprar tabaco.　　I am going to buy (a packet of) cigarettes. (*Cigarrillos* are individual cigarettes).
El tráfico es muy denso hoy.　　The traffic (which comprises many vehicles) is very heavy today.
¿Llevas mucho equipaje?　　Have you got a lot of luggage? (assuming more than one bag/suitcase)
Also: *equipo* (team), *orquesta* (orchestra) and *coro* (choir), none of which can be made up of only one member!

The use of impersonal verbs

I have christened these verbs *impersonal* because they do not work in the same way as most verbs in Spanish and English sentences. In technical terminology: *the indirect object of the verb in Spanish becomes the subject of the verb in English and the subject of the verb in Spanish becomes the direct object of the verb in English*. Any wiser?
Let's see how this works in practice! The most common verbs in question here are *gustar, encantar, apetecer* and *interesar*:
Me *gusta* el chocolate (indirect object + verb + subject)　　I *like* chocolate (subject + verb + direct object)
Me *gustan* los chocolates.　　I *like* chocolates (lots of different ones).
The grammatical formula is still the same, but the verb in Spanish has become plural to reflect the plural nature of what is being talked about or, in this case, liked. Thus the verb does not reflect the number of people affected by the action but rather the number of things in question which together form the subject of the verb:
Nos *encanta* el español.　　We *love* Spanish. (The verb is singular because it is reflecting the singular object in question (the language) not the plurality of the people).
Me *encantan* las ciencias.　　I *love* the sciences. (Plural verb with plural subject, and one person receiving the action)

127

In a similar vein:

No le *apetece* ir de compras.　She doesn't *fancy* going shopping.

No me *apetecen* las gambas.　I don't *fancy* the prawns.

Me *interesa* mucho la política.　I'm really *interested* in politics.

No me *interesan* tus peleas.　I'm not *interested* in your squabbles.

The importance of sentence structure

In speaking and in writing a language, it is important to get the sentence structure correct, perhaps more so when writing. In Spanish the sentence structure is very similar to that of English (subject + verb + object) except for one or two differences as previously mentioned:

– the grammatical inversion which takes place with the above-mentioned impersonal verbs

– the position of adjectives, generally after the noun they are describing, not before it as in English

– agreement rules which have to be made with adjectives, etc. throughout a sentence

– the fact that is not always necessary to include the subject of the verb unless doing so for emphasis. It **is** necessary to include it in English because the verb formation does not clearly state who is carrying out the action as it does in Spanish:

I do; you do; we do; they do – without the subject, it would be very difficult to know *who* was doing something!

Hago; haces; hacemos; hacen – no subject needed as the verb endings make it perfectly clear who is doing something

– my infamous ***reverse rule*** when writing/saying numbers (not a made-up rule by any means but rather a made-up name to which all my students are subjected early on in their quest to perfect their Spanish!)

The reverse rule works in the following way and is mainly applied to numbers which use a comma or a full stop/decimal point; numbers in the hundreds when the word 'and' is involved; and single and plural spellings of certain numbers:

– take the number *five and a half*: in English, if we were to write this as a decimal number, we would quite naturally write/say 5.5. However, in Spanish this would be written/ said 5,5. Conversely, in English, where we would write five thousand 5,000, in Spanish it would be written 5.000

– when the word *and* is involved in numbers up to and including 999, again the reverse rule kicks in:

52 said *fifty two* in English, said *fifty and two* in Spanish cincuenta *y* dos

184 said one hundred *and* eighty four in English, in Spanish ciento ochenta *y* cuatro

– particularly with the hundreds: 200 said *two hundred* in English but said *two hundreds* in Spanish and written as one word not two: *doscientos*

So, to recap, the reverse rule basically takes what is done/said in English and reverses it in Spanish!

The potential pitfalls of correct sentence structure can, unfortunately, involve other grammatical features, though. Here we go with some more technical terminology!

A **cleft sentence** (oración hendida) is quite common in Spanish and is usually used for contrast not emphasis. It begins with the introductory verb *ser* and is followed by the indirect object and a relative pronoun referring back to it. If a preposition is involved, it may sometimes need to be repeated:

Es a Juan a quien di el libro.   It was Juan I gave the book to.
Fue en Londres donde le conocí.   It was in London where I met him.

A **pseudo-cleft sentence** is a cleft sentence which does not begin with the verb *ser* but rather with the antecedent or even the relative pronoun or relative clause:

El perro fue quien le mordió.   It was the dog that bit him.
Quien lo hizo fue Juan.   It was Juan who did it.
Para lo que trabajo no es para ganar dinero.   I do not work just for the money.

These are more emphatic than cleft sentences.

There are also rules called *end-weight* and *end-focus* rules which can affect the natural sentence structure (and work in a similar way to the above).

An **end-weight rule** takes place when the subject is longer than the description, or vice versa, and is thus sent to the end of the sentence:
Quienes lo hicieron fueron la quinta Marquesa de Soria y su amante (otherwise: *La quinta Marquesa de Soria y su amante lo hicieron*).   It was the fifth Marquess of Soria and her lover who did it.

An **end-focus rule** takes place when the object of attention in the sentence goes to the end:
A la que oigo más quejarte eres tú.   You are the one I can hear complaining the loudest.[5]

The use of the subjunctive mood

As this is not strictly a grammar reference book but rather a Studymates guide to speaking better Spanish, I am not going to go into detail here on the formation of the subjunctive in its varying forms. Suffice to say that the subjunctive is not a tense but a mood, which can very often be remembered by thinking about the mood of the speaker (ie a subjective way of saying something). When speaking on a day-to-day basis in either English or Spanish, we tend to speak in what is known as the indicative mood. Spanish uses the subjunctive mood for certain situations, after certain words or after certain verbs. Remember:
– when the verb in the main clause is in the present indicative/future/present perfect/imperative, then the verb in the following clause is most likely to be in the present/present perfect subjunctive;
– when the verb in the main clause is in the conditional/imperfect/preterite/pluperfect, then the verb in the following clause is most likely to be in the imperfect/pluperfect subjunctive.

---

[5] Leo Hickey, former lecturer at Salford University

This will all fall into place given the following criteria:

– after certain conjunctions
When the following conjunctions introduce a new clause, the verb in that new clause should be formed in the subjunctive mood:

A fin de que.   So that, in order that.

A menos que.   Unless.

Como si.   As if.

Con tal que/con tal de que.   Provided that.

Para que.   In order that, so that.

Sin que.   Without.

When the following conjunctions introduce a new clause, the verb in that new clause may be either in the indicative **or** the subjunctive mood. The indicative mood is used if the action was completed in the past and there is no doubt about its completion. The subjunctive, on the other hand, is used if what is being expressed indicates any sort of anxious anticipation, doubt, indefiniteness, vagueness or uncertainty.

A pesar de que.   In spite of the fact that.

Así que.   As soon as, after.

Aunque.   Although, even if, even though.

Cuando.   When(ever).

De manera que.   So that, so as.

De modo que.   So that, in such a way that.

Después que/después de que.   After.

En cuanto.   As soon as.

Hasta que.   Until.

Luego que.   As soon as, after.

Mientras.   While, as long as.

Siempre que.   Whenever, provided that.

-after certain adverbs:
Acaso, *quizá(s)* and *tal vez*, which all mean 'perhaps', 'maybe'.

– after certain indefinite expressions:
Cualquier/cualquiera/cualesquier/cualesquiera.   Whatever, whichever, any.

Cuandoquiera.   Whenever.

Dondequiera. Wherever.
Adondequiera. To wherever.
Quienquiera/quienesquiera. Whoever.

– after certain impersonal expressions:
Basta que. It is enough that, it is sufficient that.
Conviene que. It is fitting that, it is proper that.
Importa que. It is important that.
Más vale que. It is better that.
Es aconsejable que. It is advisable that.

– after verbs or expressions that indicate denial, doubt or lack of belief, and uncertainty:

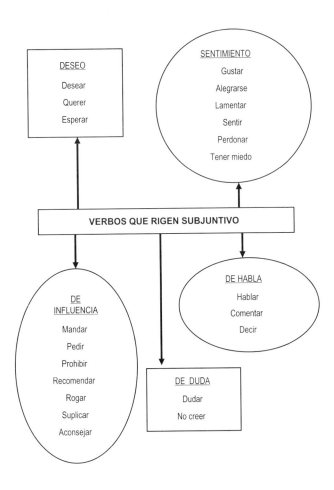

Dudar que.   To doubt that.

Negar que.   To deny that.

No creer que.   Not to believe that.

Es dudoso que.   It is doubtful that.

Es incierto que.   It is uncertain that.

Hay duda que.   There is doubt that.

No es cierto que.   It is not certain that.

No estar seguro que.   Not to be sure that.

– after verbs or expressions that indicate an emotion:

Estar contento que.   To be happy that, to be pleased that.

Estar feliz que.   To be happy that.

Estar triste que.   To be sad that.

Alegrarse (de) que.   To be glad that.

Sentir que.   To regret that, to feel sorry that.

– after certain verbs that imply a wish or desire that something be done (usually by someone else), including a command, order, preference, advice, permission, request, plea, insistence and suggestion:

Aconsejar.   To advise.

Decir.   To tell (someone to do something).

Desear.   To want, to wish.

Mandar.   To order, to command.

Pedir.   To ask, to request.

Preferir.   To prefer.

Prohibir.   To forbid, to prohibit, to ban.

Querer.   To want, to wish.

Rogar.   To beg, to request.

Sugerir.   To suggest.

– after *¡que.....!* in order to indirectly express a wish, an order or a command in the third person singular or plural:

¡Que lo haga María!   Let Maria do it!

¡Que aproveche!   Enjoy your meal!

-after *¡Ojalá que . . . !* to express the idea of 'If only . . . !':

¡Ojalá que llueva!   If only it would rain!

¡Ojalá que se vayan!   If only they would leave!

– after an indefinite or negative antecedent:

The reason why a verb in the subjunctive mood is needed here is because the person or thing desired may possibly not exist or, if it does, you may never come across them/it:

Busco un libro que sea interesante. I am looking for a book that is interesting (but I may never find one).

¿Conoces a alguien quien tenga la paciencia de enseñar la flauta a mi hija? Do you know of anyone who has the patience to teach my daughter to play the flute? (They may not exist or you may not know of them.)

No había nadie quien supiera la respuesta correcta Nobody knew the correct answer (or at least I could not find anyone who knew).

The use of prepositions and their associated verbs

A preposition is a word that connects words and, according to the thought expressed in the sentence, serves to indicate the relationship between the words. Prepositions can also serve to position a noun (hence their name); examples in English include *on, in, at, under, by, next to* and *on top of.*

Common prepositions in Spanish are:

A   at, to
Ante   before, in the presence of
Bajo   under
Con   *with*
Contra   against
De   of, from
Desde   after, from, since
Durante   during
En   in, on
Entre   among, between
Hacia   towards
Hasta   until, up to, as far as
Menos   except
Para   for, in order to
Por   by, for
Salvo   except, save
Sin   without
Sobre   on, upon, over, above

Tras   after, behind

Common prepositional phrases in Spanish are:

Acerca de   about
Además de   in adition to, besides
Alrededor de   around
Antes de   before
Antes de nada   *before anything*
Antes de nadie   before anyone
Cerca de   near
Con rumbo a   in the direction of
Debajo de   underneath
Delante de   in front of
Dentro de   within, inside
Después de   after
Detrás de   behind
En contra de   against, opposed to
En cuanto a   as far as (something is concerned)
En lugar de   in place of, instead of
En medio de   in the middle of
En vez de   instead of
Encima de   on top of, upon
Enfrente de   opposite
Frente a   in front of
Fuera de   outside of
Junto a   next to
Lejos de   far from
Por valor de   worth

Note: many of these prepositional phrases would not be prepositional without the addition of *de* but rather adverbial.

Many verbs which are followed by a preposition in English are also followed by a preposition in Spanish (albeit sometimes a different one); some verbs in English which are **not** followed by a preposition **do** have one in Spanish; and some verbs in English are followed by a preposition but when translated into Spanish, they are **not**. The following list of verbs is one containing common verbal constructions in Spanish which use the prepositions *a, con, de, en, por* and *para*:

Aburrirse de (+ infin). To get bored with doing.

Acabar con algo/alguien. To put an end to something/finish with someone.

Acabar de (+ infin). To have just done.

Acabar por (+ infin). To end up doing.

Acercarse a algo/alguien. To approach something/someone.

Acordarse de algo/alguien/de (+ infin). To remember something/someone/doing.

Acostumbrarse a algo/alguien/a (+ infin). To get used to something/someone/doing.

Acusar a alguien de algo/de (+ perfect infin). To accuse someone of something/of doing/having done.

Advertir a alguien de algo. To notify/warn someone about something.

Aficionarse a algo/a (+ infin). To grow fond of something/of doing.

Alegrarse de algo/de (+ perfect infin). To be glad about something/of doing/having done.

Alejarse de algo/alguien. To move away from something/someone.

Amenazar a alguien con algo/con (+ infin). To threaten someone with something/to do.

Animar a alguien a (+ infin). To encourage someone to do.

Apresurarse a (+ infin). To hurry to do.

Aprender a (+ infin). To learn to do.

Aprovecharse de algo/alguien. To take advantage of something/someone.

Aproximarse a algo/alguien. To approach something/someone.

Asistir a algo. To attend/be at something.

Asomarse a/por. To lean out of.

Asombrarse de (+ infin). To be surprised at doing.

Atreverse a (+ infin). To dare to do.

Avergonzarse de algo/alguien/de (+ perfect infin). To be ashamed of something/someone/of doing/having done.

Ayudar a alguien a (+ infin). To help someone to do.

Bajarse de (place/vehicle).   To get off/out of.
Burlarse de alguien.   To make fun of someone.

Cansarse de algo/alguien/de (+ infin).   To tire of something/someone/doing.
Carecer de algo.   To lack something.
Cargar de algo.   To load with something.
Casarse con alguien.   To marry someone/get married to someone.
Cesar de (+ infin).   To stop doing.
Chocar con algo.   To crash/bump into something.
Comenzar a (+ infin).   To begin to do.
Comparar con algo/alguien.   To compare with something/someone.
Consentir en (+ infin).   To agree to do.
Consistir en (+ infin).   To consist of doing.
Constar de algo.   To consist of something.
Contar con algo/alguien.   To rely on something/someone.
Convenir en (+ infin).   To agree to do.

Dar a.   To face.
Dar con algo.   To find/come upon something.
Dar con alguien.   To meet/run into/come across/find someone.
Dar contra.   *To hit against.*
Dar de beber/comer a alguien.   To give someone something to drink/eat.
Dar en.   To hit/strike against.
Dar por (+ past participle).   To consider.
Darse cuenta de algo.   To realise something.
Dejar de (+ infin).   To stop doing.
Depender de algo/alguien.   To depend on something/someone.
Despedirse de alguien.   To say goodbye to someone.
Dirigirse a (place)/*alguien.*   To head for/address someone.
Disponerse a (+ infin).   To get ready to do.

Empezar a (+ infin).   To begin to do.
Empezar por (+ infin).   To begin by doing.

Encontrarse con alguien.   To meet someone (by chance).

Enfadarse con alguien.   To get annoyed with someone.

Enseñar a alguien a (+ infin).   To teach someone to.

Enterarse de algo.   To find out about something.

Entrar en (+ place).   To enter/go into.

Esperar a (+ infin).   To wait until.

Estar a punto de (+ infin).   To be about to do.

Estar de acuerdo con algo/alguien.   To agree with something/someone.

Estar para (+ infin)/(+ noun).   To be about to/in the mood for.

Estar por.   To be in favour of.

Fiarse de algo/alguien.   To trust something/someone.

Fijarse en algo/alguien.   To notice something/someone.

Hablar con alguien.   To talk to someone.

Hacer caso a alguien.   To pay attention to someone.

Hacer daño a alguien.   To hurt someone.

Hacer el favor de (+ infin).   To please/kindly do.

Hacer el papel de.   To play the role of.

Hartarse de algo/alguien/de (+ infin).   To get fed up with something/someone/doing.

Interesarse por algo/alguien.   To be interested in something/someone.

Invitar a alguien a (+ infin).   To invite someone to do.

Ir de compras.   To go shopping.

Jugar a (+ sports/game).   To play.

Luchar por algo/por (+ infin).   To fight/strive for something/to do.

Llegar a (+ place)/*a* (+ infin).   To reach/manage to do.

Llenar de algo.   To fill with something.

Negarse a (+ infin).   To refuse to do.

Obligar a alguien a (+ infin).   To make someone do.

Ocuparse de algo/alguien.   To attend to something/take care of someone.

Oler a algo.   To smell of something.

Olvidarse de algo/alguien/de (+ infin). To forget something/someone/to do.
Oponerse a algo/a (+ infin). To be opposed to something/to doing.

Parecerse a algo/alguien. To resemble something/someone.
Pensar en algo/alguien/en (+ infin). To think about something/someone/doing.
Preguntar por alguien. To ask for/after/about someone.
Preocuparse de/por algo/alguien. To worry about something/someone.
Prepararse a (*+infin*). To prepare to do.

Quedar en (+ infin). To agree to do.
Quedar por (+ infin). To remain to be done.
Quejarse de algo. To complain about something.

Referirse a algo. To refer to something.
Reírse de algo/alguien. To laugh at something/someone.
Rodear de. To surround with.
Romper a (+ infin). To (suddenly) start to do.

Salir de (+ place). To leave.
Sentarse a (+ infin). To sit down to do.
Ser aficionado a. To be a fan of.
Ser amable con alguien. To be kind to someone.
Subir(se) a (+ vehicle/place). To get on/into/climb.
Servir de algo a alguien. To be useful to/serve someone as something.
Servir para algo/para (+ infin). To be good as something/for doing.
Servirse de algo. To use something.
Soñar con algo/alguien/con (+ infin). To dream about something/someone/doing.
Sorprenderse de algo. To be surprised at something.

Tardar en (+ infin). To take time to do.
Tener ganas de (+ infin). To feel like doing.
Tener gusto en (+ infin). To be glad to.
Tener miedo de algo. To be afraid of something.
Terminar por (+ infin). To end by doing.

Tirar de algo.   To pull something.

Trabajar de (+ occupation).   To work as.

Trabajar en (+ place).   To work at/in.

Traducir a (+ language).   To translate into.

Tratar de (+ infin).   To try to do.

Tratarse de algo/alguien/de (+ infin).   To be a question of something/about someone/about doing.

Vacilar en (+ infin).   To hesitate to do.

Volver a (+ infin).   To do again.

The following list is of verbs which, in English, carry a preposition but do **not** do so in Spanish:

Aprobar algo.   To approve of something.

Buscar algo/a alguien.   To look for something/someone.

Desear algo.   To long for something.

Escuchar algo.   To listen to something.

Esperar algo/a alguien.   To wait for something/someone.

Impedir que alguien haga algo.   To prevent someone from doing something.

Mirar algo.   To look at something.

Pagar algo.   To pay for something.

Pedir algo.   To ask for something.

Presidir algo.   To preside over something.

Reprocharle algo a alguien.   To reproach someone for something.

From this, it should be clear that in English it is perfectly possible to change the meaning of a verb by placing a preposition after it. However, in Spanish this is not the case and very often a completely different verb would be required to translate a variety of meanings. Careful dictionary usage required at all times!

Specific translation pitfalls

Translating word for word from English into Spanish is a definite no-no as you become more at ease with how the language works and the possible linguistic situations you may unwittingly find yourself in! The following presents a list of grammatical points which, when mastered, will sharpen your rendering of spoken (and written) Spanish.

– Some verbs have no preposition in English yet are translated with one in Spanish:

To address.   *Dirigirse a.*
To approach.   *Acercarse a.*
To arrange to do.   *Quedarse en.*
To attend.   *Asistir a.*
To climb.   *Subir a.*
To consider doing.   *Pensar en .*
To dare to do.   *Atreverse a.*
To end up doing.   *Acabarse por.*
To enter.   *Entrar en.*
To finish.   *Terminar de.*
To forget.   *Olvidarse de.*
To hesitate.   *Vacilar en.*
To hurry.   *Apresurarse a.*
To lack.   *Carecer de.*
To leave (a place).   *Salir de.*
To marry.   *Casarse con.*
To meet.   *Encontrarse con.*
To notice.   *Fijarse en.*
To play (a game/sport).   *Jugar a.*
To pull.   *Tirar de.*
To reach.   *Llegar a.*
To realise.   *Darse cuenta de.*
To refuse.   *Negarse a.*
To remember.   *Acordarse de.*
To resemble.   *Parecerse a.*
To trust.   *Fiarse de.*

– Some verbs are followed by a preposition (phrasal verbs) in English and translated without one in Spanish:

To approve of.   *Aprobar.*
To ask for.   *Pedir.*
To fall down.   *Caerse.*
To give in.   *Ceder.*
To listen to.   *Escuchar.*
To long for.   *Desear.*
To look at.   *Mirar.*
To look for.   *Buscar.*

To pay for.   *Pagar.*
To preside over.   *Presidir.*
To prevent from.   *Impedir.*
To reproach for.   *Reprochar.*
To run away.   *Huir.*
To wait for.   *Esperar.*

– A word which is singular in English may be plural in Spanish or vice versa:

Tomar unas vacaciones.   To take a holiday.

Había mucha gente.   There were a lot of people.

Este pantalón es mi favorito.   These are my favourite trousers.

– Spanish has no equivalent of the possessive indicator, namely — 's or — s':

El coche de mi padre.   My father's car.

Los derechos de los padres.   Parents' rights.

The rule here is that the object you are talking about comes first followed by any form of adjectival description and finally to whom it belongs:

El coche nuevo de mi hermano.   My brother's new car (literally: the car – new – of my brother).

Helping you learn

Progress checks

1 Translate useful English phrases into Spanish, bearing in mind all relevant points of grammar, and check the topics covered in this chapter.
2 Read in Spanish as often as possible, trying to spot potential problems.
3 When listening to/reading in Spanish, try to concentrate on the usage of any potentially problematic words.
4 List different ways of saying the same thing and check them with a dictionary.

Discussion points

1 Always take the opportunity to ask native speakers for explanations and clarifications.
2 Know when to use particular words and expressions.
3 Why are there so many rules? Do you agree that your own language has just as many difficulties?

Practical assignments

1 Discuss problems and difficulties encountered by fellow students.
2 Always try to spot which words and expressions are used and in which context.
3 Never miss the opportunity to visit a Spanish-speaking country.

Study tips

1 The secret of 'fluency' is that practice makes perfect.
2 Use all the Spanish you know at every opportunity.
3 Extend and perfect your Spanish every day.

Websites
for students
of Spanish

One-minute summary

Nowadays use of the Internet is almost second nature to many people to gain access to an invaluably useful resource on virtually any subject matter. The following websites may help you in your quest for knowledge in Spanish but please note that neither the author nor the publisher is responsible for content or opinions expressed on the sites listed. The websites given are merely intended to serve as starting blocks for students and, indeed, please remember that the Internet is probably changing as you read this and that web links may come and go. If you have any websites which you feel would be of use in future editions of this book, please write to Carole Shepherd, c/o Studymates (address on the back cover) or alternatively you are welcome to surf a free selection of useful and readymade links for students on the Studymates website:

http://www.studymates.co.uk

Search engines

http://www.yahoo.es (Yahoo search engine for Spain)
http://www.ole.es/ (Spanish search engine)
http://www.rediris.es/doc/buscadores.es.html (extensive list of search engines and sites)
http://www.google.com
http://www.guiame.net
http://uk.altavista.com
http://www.lycos.com

http://www.sol.com (Spain Online)

http://www.altamira.net

For students

http://www.sgci.mec.es/uk/Pub/tecla (a text magazine written by the Consejería de Educación for learners and teachers of Spanish. Appears weekly during the UK academic year with activities at three different levels. Part of an initiative by the Spanish Government to promote the Spanish language and culture throughout the world)

http://www.vokabel.com (vocabulary training exercises)

http://www.ontheline.org.uk (has French and Spanish materials)

http://www.livjm.ac.uk/language/

http://www.bbc.co.uk/education_webguide/pkg_main.p_home

http://www.schoolzone.co.uk/ (information resource with links to hundreds of websites for Spanish and many other languages)

http://www.quia.com (games, puzzles and quizzes)

http://www.well.ac.uk/teacher/wellproj/training.htm (grammar practice activities designed by Juan Ramón de Arana of Ursinus College)

http://www.bton.ac.uk/slweb/recursos/recursos.html (Hispanic resources supplied by Brighton University)

http://hum.port.ac.uk/slas/splat/firstpage.htm (Hispanic resources supplied by Portsmouth University)

http://www.hull.ac.uk/cti/langsite/hispanic.htm (Hispanic resources supplied by the CTI Centre at Hull University)

http://www.SiSpain.org//spanish/index.html (extensive database)

http://www.cec-spain.org.uk (Consejería de Educación, London)

http://cvc.cervantes.es/portada.htm (good for cultural information)

http://cvc.cervantes.es/aula/lecturas/ (extracts from novels at three levels)

http://www.el-castellano.com/ (updated daily with latest news on the Spanish language) http://Foreignword.com (online dictionary)

http://www.zonaele.com (for students and teachers of Spanish)

http://www.uned.es/lidil/espextr/index.htm (Spanish course for foreigners)

http://descubremadrid.com/aprende_espanol.asp

http://www.donquijote.org/Spanish (Spanish in Spain, Mexico and Peru)

http://www.studyspanish.com/index.htm (useful for students and teachers with clear exercises and explanations)

http://aries17.uwaterloo.ca/lando/verbos/con-jugador.html (aimed at adult learners to help with conjugation of verbs. Mostly in Spanish so you need to be familiar with Spanish grammatical terms)

http://www3.anaya.es/diccionario/diccionar.htm (online dictionary with definitions in Spanish)

http://www.modlangs.co.uk (authentic texts and worksheets)

http://www.linguaweb.co.uk (online language learning resources)

http://babelfish.altavista.digital.com/cgi-bin/translate? (translates with varying success into French, German and Spanish and vice versa)

http://www.umsl.edu/mocsproj/mundosp.html

http://www.uupimsn.com/chat

http://amistad.ciudadfutura.com/foros

http://www.aries17.waterloo.co/lando/verbos/con_jugador.html

Sites about Spain/Latin America

http://www.sgci.mec.es/uk (web page of the Consejería de Educación UK and Ireland.)

http://www.la_moncloa.es (web page of the Moncloa palace, seat of the Office of the President of the Government. Provides links with all the Spanish Government offices and the Spanish Autonomous Comunities)

http://www.mec.es (Spanish Ministry for Education, Culture and Sport. Provides information about education in Spain, schools and universities, courses on Spanish as a foreign language, etc. There are also links with museums and other cultural institutions)

http://www.tourspain.es (Spanish Tourism web page)

http://www.mtas.es (Ministerio de Trabajo y Asuntos Exteriores)

http://www.red2000.com/spain/1index.html

http://donde.uji.es/ (especially for cities and regions)

http://www.cibercentro.com/index.html

http://www.lanic.utexas.edu

http://www.softguides.com/ (copious information about Madrid)

http://www.odci.gov/cia/publications/pubs.html (basic data on most countries in the world, includes maps. Produced by the US Central Intelligence Agency)

http://www.state.gov/www/issues/economic/trade_reports/index.html (country reports on economic policy and trade practices. Contains summary text on economic situation in approximately 90 countries. Compiled by US Department of State)

http://constitucion.rediris.es/codigo/complementario/civil/cc (Spanish law)

http://europa.eu.int/comm/index_es.htm (every kind of information about the EU)

http://www.europarl.es/

http://www.euroinfo.cce.es/index-es.html

http://www.docuweb.ca/SiSpain/ (multilingual site produced by the Spanish Ministry of Foreign Affairs)

http://www.addeva.co.uk (information on Spain)

http://www.Spanisharriba.co.uk (news from Spain, Mexico and Latin America)

http://www.boleadora.com/andes.htm

http://www.sololiteratura.com/index.htm

http://www.turning-pages.com/mafalda/mafalda_es.htm

Media online

http://www.elpais.es/ (El País, the biggest national daily newspaper)

http://w3.el-mundo.es/ (El Mundo, daily newspaper)

http://www.abc.es/ (ABC, daily newspaper)

http://www2.vanguardia.es/ (La Vanguardia, daily newspaper)

http://www.rtve.es/rne/index.htm (Radio Nacional de España)

http://www.antena3tv.es/ (Antena 3 TV channel)

http://www.dur.ac.uk (links information and newspapers)

http://www.bc.encomix.es

http://www.oei.es/medios.htm

http://www.news.bbc.co.uk/hi/spanish/news/

To get a country by country listing of online newspapers throughout the world try World Wide List of Online Newspapers at:

http://www.webwombat.comau/intercom/newsprs/

Appendix

A brief linguistic history of a beautiful language

The Spanish language forms part of a group of languages called the 'Romance' languages which all derive from Latin. Other languages in this group include Catalan, Portuguese, French, Italian and Romanian. With the rule of the Romans established in the Iberian Peninsula towards the end of the third century BC, local languages became less frequently used in favour of Latin, but one of the pre-Romance languages, *el vascuence*, is still in use today in *el País Vasco* (the Basque country). Some lexical items from pre-Roman times still exist in the Spanish we speak today: examples are *cama* (bed), *perro* (dog) and *vega* (plain/area of flat land). *El vascuence* itself embellished the Spanish language more than some of the others did because it never disappeared: surnames such as *García* and *Ayala* and forenames such as *Iñigo* and *Jimena* are of Basque origin. However, it was Latin which ruled the linguistic day, but a Latin which was itself full of Greek borrowings: *escuela* (school), *cuerda* (rope), *gobernar* (to govern), *bodega* (wine cellar), *menta* (mint), *ancla* (anchor), *huérfano* (orphan) and *idea* (idea), to mention but a few.

With the fall of the Roman Empire came the rise of the Visigoths and the inevitable influx of words with a Germanic origin: *guerra* (war), *robar* (to rob/steal), *guardar* (to keep), *falda* (skirt), *rico* (rich) and *fresco* (fresh/new) can be added to the list. Yet the biggest influence was yet to come with the gradual conquest of the Peninsula by the Moors from the beginning of the eighth century, an invasion which was to last almost eight centuries until the fall of Granada in 1492. The Arabic influence was overwhelming not only linguistically but culturally too and eventually Castilian Spanish (*el castellano*) was born, taken to the Americas and it took its rightful place amongst the world's leading languages.

Arabic brought some 4,000 words to the Spanish language and these can be put into various categories:

Agriculture: *alcachofa* (artichoke), *zanahoria* (carrot), *azúcar* (sugar), *algodón* (cotton), *berenjena* (aubergine)

Commerce: *tarifa* (tariff), *aduana* (customs)

Housing: *aldea* (small village/hamlet), *almohada* (pillow), *albañil* (bricklayer/mason), *azulejo* (tile)

Administration: *alcalde* (mayor)

Mathematics: *cifra* (figure/number), *cero* (zero), *algebra* (algebra)

Science: *alquimia* (alchemy), *alcohol* (alcohol), *jarabe* (syrup), *cenit* (zenith)

Place and river names: *la Mancha, Guadalajara, Guadalquivir, Gibraltar, Calatayud*

Note that the much-used words *ojalá* (if only) and *tarea* (task/chore) are also of Arabic origin.

With the conquest of America came a knowledge of plants and animals, in particular, which were previously unknown in Europe. Many local words were adopted into Spanish in order to express these novelties and from Spanish the words made their way into other European languages: *tomate* (tomato), *chocolate* (chocolate), *canoa* (canoe), *batata* (sweet potato), *caimán* (alligator/caiman), *tabaco* (tobacco) and *hamaca* (hammock) are examples. These words first entered the Spanish language during the 16th century when Spain was the most powerful country in Europe and to speak Spanish was essential for anyone of standing.

Today, Spanish, itself enhanced with influences from French, Italian and English, is spoken as a first language by more than 300 million people in at least 20 countries. It is the most studied foreign language in the United States and increasingly so in Europe and Japan. Spanish is a great literary language with many famous writers, some of whom are Nobel laureates, and there are hundreds of magazines and newspapers published in the language, not only in the countries where it is officially spoken but also where there are large numbers of Hispanic communities such as in the USA. In Latin America, there are millions of people whose mother tongue is actually an indigenous language but who use Spanish as their official means of communication. Spanish is one of the official languages of the United Nations and the European Union and is also used at many an international congress. Spanish is now probably the fourth most widely spoken language in the world after Chinese, English and, possibly, Hindi.

Index

English listing
and, 48
be, **25**, 88, 90
begin, 4
brown, 33
but, 48
catch, 3
cook, 2
country, 40
die, 18
do/make, 28, 89
face, **41**, 42
fight, 16
for, **49**, 51
free, **34**, 35
give, 87
go, **14**, 89
goodbye, 52, **80–81**
half, **42**, 43
have, **26**, 27, 91
help, **43**, 44
know, 23
leave, **6**, 14
like, **12**, 127
miss, **10**, 11, 19
need/require, 19
old, **35**, 36
or, 51
perhaps, 131
play, 15
put, **20**, 90
say, 5
slim, 37
so, 51
sorry, **81–83**
speed, **44**, 45
spend, **12**, 61
stay/remain, 7, **90**
take, 3, 4, **27**, 89, 92, 98
throw, **7**, 88, 101
time, **45**, 46
try, **21**, 23, 68
use, **29**, 49
want, 12, 19, **23**, 133

work, 46
wrong, 38

"four-letter" words, 97–102

false friends, 55–70
   acostar, 55;
   actual, 56;
   advertir, 63;
   *agonía, 19, **64**;*
   anciano, 56;
   antiguo, 56;
   apología, 64;
   arena, 56;
   asistir, 56;
   atender, 55;
   auditorio, 55;
   bachiller, 63;
   bagaje, 63;
   bala, 63;
   barraca, 63;
   bizarro, 63;
   bizcocho, 55;
   campo, 55;
   calificar, 65;
   carbón, 55;
   cargo, 65;
   carpeta, 55;
   carta, 57;
   chanza, 65;
   chocar, 57;
   collar, 57;
   colorado, 65;
   cómodo, 57;
   complexión, 65;
   condescender, 65;
   conferencia, 60;
   confianza, 57;
   confidencia, 57;
   constipado, 57;
   consulta, 57;
   contestar, 58;
   convenir, 58;
   decepción, 58;

delito, 66;
desgracia, 66;
desmayo, 58;
destituir, 66;
destreza, 66;
devolver, 58;
diario, 58;
disgusto, 66;
distinto, 66;
divisar, 58;
divulgación, 66;
editor, 58;
efectivamente, 58;
embarazada, 58;
emocionante, 59;
equivocar, 66;
esperar, 59;
espina, 59;
eventual, 59;
éxito, 59;
extenuar, 66;
fábrica, 60;
genial, 60;
idioma, 60;
injuria, 67;
intoxicado, 67;
jubilarse, 60;
labrador, 67;
largo, 60;
lectura, 60;
librería, 60;
lujuria, 67;
maleta, 60;
mantel, 61;
mayor, 61;
mesura, 67;
noticia, 61;
oración, 67;
ordinario, 67;
palo, 67;
pariente, 61;
particular, 61;
pasar, 61;
pastel, 61;
pinchar, 68;
pretender, 68;

profesor, 61;
prospecto, 68;
pupilo, 68;
rato, 68;
realizar, 62;
recordar, 62;
refrán, 68;
regalar, 62;
remover, 68;
restar, 69;
sancionar, 69;
sano, 62;
sensible, 62;
simpático, 62;
soportar, 62;
suburbio, 69;
suceder, 69;
suspender, 62;
tabla, 69;
tinta, 62;
tormenta, 63;
trampa, 63;
vaso, 63;
voluble, 69

Spanish listing

ahora bien, 116
apodo, 79
capicúa, 83
chisme, 79
churro, 83
coba, 79
criollo, 84
diga, 84
dios, 79
fulano, 80
funesto, 80
gringo, 84
guay, 80
jesús, 80
juerga, 84
machismo, 84
madrugada, 84
movida, 85
olé, 85
paella, 85

pasota, 85
piropo, 85
santo, 86
seseo, 86
tapas, 86
tarde, 86
tertulia, 87
trámites, 80
tropecientos, 80
tutear, 87

Grammatical listing
accents, 108–110
adjectives, 25, **123–128**
articles (definite, indefinite, neuter), 116–123

collective nouns, 126–127
exclamations, **73–77**, 111
idioms, sayings and proverbs, 87–95
impersonal verbs, 11, 14, 19, **127–128**
personal 'a', 115–116
prepositions, 134–142
pronunciation, **104–106**, 109–111
repetition, 72–73
sentence structure, 128–130
subjunctive, 130–134
tag questions, 71

About the author

Carole Shepherd is a qualified teacher and Head of Spanish at Virgo Fidelis Convent Senior School in Croydon and has taught French and Spanish in England since 1991. Carole taught English as a foreign language in Madrid over a period of seven years, four of which were spent living in the Spanish capital. She is also the editor of *Hands on GCSE Spanish: Reading and Responding*, published by Bermes Language Resources.